Resounding Praise for Roy Peter Clarke's
Tell It Like It Is

"In a world with too much propaganda, confusion, and misinformation, Roy Peter Clark offers us a kind of North Star. His indispensable new book makes an urgent case for clarity, honesty, and conviction. Clark once again teaches us something crucial. We should all be aiming to write with purpose, for the public good. Now more than ever, we need this book."

— Diana K. Sugg, Pulitzer Prize–winning reporter, *Baltimore Sun*

"Required reading. With engaging anecdotes and examples from across many disciplines, legendary writing coach Roy Peter Clark shows us how to perfect our craft for the common good. I'll be handing this book out to all the writers in my life who need guidance and, more important, encouragement and inspiration."

— Tom Huang, assistant managing editor, *Dallas Morning News*

"Roy Peter Clark shares a toolbox for achieving clear and honest communication that's invaluable for anyone who is — or wants to be — a public writer."

— Colette Bancroft, copy desk chief and book critic, *Tampa Bay Times*

"If you write public words for the greater good (talks, articles, letters to the editor, even Covid-test instructions), this elegant and handy manual will help you understand your topic imaginatively and deeply, then cast it as an engaging human story, and, finally, edit with dozens of Clark's sensible and dynamic writing tips. I'm hardly alone among authors who regard Roy Peter Clark as America's foremost (and funniest) writing teacher."

— Mark Kramer, coeditor of *Telling True Stories* and founder of the Nieman Program on Narrative Journalism at Harvard University

"With insight, wit, and generosity, Roy Peter Clark's *Tell It Like It Is* gives us a fresh, necessary set of writing tools: essential tools for truth-telling we urgently need in the struggle against disinformation and demagoguery, and in defense of democratic self-rule and fact-based reality."

— Paul A. Kramer, Vanderbilt University

"There is no antidote to confusion and misinformation more powerful than *Tell It Like It Is.* Anyone seeking to make their writing more straightforward, compelling, and memorable needs to read this book."

— Sewell Chan, editor in chief, *Texas Tribune*

"There may be no more timely, thoughtful, useful, and needed book in this age of disinformation and lying in public media than *Tell It Like It Is.* If you are eagerly awaiting advice and counsel on how to write your way out of the muck and mire that is our media public sphere, this is the book for you. Clark brings his experience, integrity, humor, and brilliance to bear in all aspects of his work as a writer and teacher. I hope this book gets on the shelf of every human being with a pen or a computer."

—Arthur L. Caplan, Mitty Professor of Bioethics, New York University Grossman School of Medicine

"Roy Peter Clark is to clear writing what Windex is to glass."

—Neil Brown, president of the Poynter Institute and co-chair of the Pulitzer Prize Board

"*Tell It Like It Is* offers a valuable and timely perspective on writing, where it fits into career and life, and why it matters to communicate with both clarity and nuance."

—Katharine Gammon, Nieman Storyboard

"Clark highlights how any of us—all of us—can be called to communicate with our fellow citizens through writing. With his signature deft humor and inspiring observations, Roy offers a road map for upping your writing game that is actually fun to follow, while also making the case that clear public writing is a civic good that should be encouraged and applauded—particularly when it cuts through misinformation or willful disinformation. Best of all, Roy's own sterling personal attributes—his patience, kindness, good nature, and earnest desire to help anyone aspiring to get better as a writer—shine through on every page. *Tell It Like It Is* is insightful, entertaining, and one of the best books on writing I have ever read—guaranteed to galvanize you into crafting sentences and stories before you've even put it down."

—Eric Deggans, TV critic and media analyst, National Public Radio

Also by Roy Peter Clark

Murder Your Darlings: And Other Gentle Writing Advice from Aristotle to Zinsser

The Art of X-Ray Reading: How the Secrets of 25 Great Works of Literature Will Improve Your Writing

How to Write Short: Word Craft for Fast Times

Help! for Writers: 210 Solutions to the Problems Every Writer Faces

The Glamour of Grammar: A Guide to the Magic and Mystery of Practical English

Writing Tools: 55 Essential Strategies for Every Writer

Tell It Like It Is

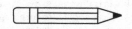

A Guide to Clear and Honest Writing

Roy Peter Clark

Little, Brown Spark
New York Boston London

This book is dedicated to my clear and honest bride, Karen Major Clark, who has been my essential guide for more than fifty years.

Little, Brown Spark
Hachette Book Group
1290 Avenue of the Americas, New York, NY 10104
littlebrownspark.com

Originally published in hardcover by Little, Brown Spark, April 2023
First Little, Brown Spark paperback edition, April 2024

Little, Brown Spark is an imprint of Little, Brown and Company, a division of Hachette Book Group, Inc. The Little, Brown Spark name and logo are trademarks of Hachette Book Group, Inc.

ISBN 9780316317139 (hc) / 9780316317238 (pb)
LCCN 2023931172

10 9 8 7 6 5 4 3 2 1

CW

Printed in Canada

CONTENTS

Part III: Honesty and Candor

Tell it like it is, don't be ashamed to let your conscience be your guide....

— "Tell It Like It Is," sung by Aaron Neville,
lyrics by Lee Diamond and George Davis

By the way, you all write for a living. I haven't seen any of you explain the supply chain very well. No, no, I'm not being critical. I'm being deadly earnest.... This is a confusing time.

— President Joe Biden to reporters at the
White House, November 6, 2021

I would also like to thank the journalists who put their lives at risk to provide information. Thank you, brothers and sisters, for this service that allows us to be close to the tragedy of that population and enables us to assess the cruelty of a war. #Ukraine #Peace.

— Pope Francis, Twitter, March 6, 2022

PREFACE

The darker and more dystopian the future appears, the more influential public writers become. But with so much content vying for our attention, and so much misinformation and propaganda polluting public discourse, how can writers break through the noise to inform an increasingly busy, stressed, and overwhelmed audience?

In *Tell It Like It Is* I do my best to offer a succinct and practical guide to writing with clarity, honesty, and conviction. By analyzing stellar writing examples from a diverse collection of public writers, I highlight and explain the tools journalists, scientists, economists, fact-checkers, and even storytellers and poets use to engage, inform, and hook readers, and how best to deploy them in a variety of contexts. In doing so, I offer answers to some of the most pressing questions facing writers today:

How do I make hard facts—about pandemics, war,

natural disasters, economics, social justice, the environment—easier reading?

How do I make boring but important stuff interesting? How do I get readers to pay attention to what they need to know?

How do I take responsibility for what readers know and understand, not just by making information available to the public, but by making it comprehensible, even handy?

How do I contribute to a culture of writing and communication that serves as an antidote to lies, misinformation, and vicious propaganda?

How do I bring light into the darkness? Hope into the hearts and minds of readers?

I may be best known for writing books about writing. But during the pandemic I felt compelled to write about the troubles we all were experiencing. My hometown newspaper, the *Tampa Bay Times*, and its website published my columns on Sundays. Some essays were about issues and controversies, some with life-and-death consequences. Many more were whimsical, providing relief from the darker news, or hope that we all could survive the day and that things would get better. In that sense, *Tell It Like It Is* is a heartfelt, practical, and, I hope, engaging guide to public writing in unprecedented times—and an urgently needed remedy for a dangerously confused world.

This is the seventh book since 2006 that I have worked on with editor Tracy Behar and her helpful and often joyful colleagues at Little, Brown. More than a half-million of these books—on writing, grammar, journalism, reading, and literature — are now in print. *Tell It Like It Is* brings a new urgency to my mission, first stated in *Writing Tools*, to help create a nation of public writers.

Tell It Like It Is

INTRODUCTION

The Bright Light of Public Writing

In great moments of crisis, we need public servants to help us through. Among the most important are writers who let us know what is going on and help us understand what it all means and what we can do about it. Some of these public writers would identify as journalists or at least, in their humility, as reporters or editors. But not all of them would. Some we might call researchers, scholars, speech writers, advocates—even novelists, scriptwriters, poets, and moviemakers.

Ideological polarization, fueled by paranoia and xenophobia, has scarred our political life since the birth of our republic. It has returned to cast a shadow upon all forms of learning and expertise. Under the broad title of "elites," scientists and medical workers, college educators, journalists and other media figures, writers, librarians, school board members, even elementary school teachers, have found themselves under attack. While fanatics have sparked such attacks for centuries, social media now provides the fuel to turn conflagrations into national infernos.

In such an environment, people of goodwill must recommit themselves to the struggle against ignorance, injustice, and intolerance. When we write for the public good, we often find reasons for neutrality and impartiality. But being neutral about some things does not require us to be neutral about everything.

Tell It Like It Is offers support to public writers and aspiring public writers — to any writer who wants to perfect their craft for the common good. I learned as a young child in Catholic school that the three great virtues are faith, hope, and love. My epistle to you embraces those three and adds two more that should glow in the hearts of every public writer: clarity and honesty.

Clarity results from the careful exercise of craft, often using shorter words, sentences, and paragraphs at the points of greatest complexity. It comes from a purposeful attention to language, voice, and the pace of information. It can come from powerful storytelling in the public interest. Clarity requires the writer's embrace of a mission and purpose: to take responsibility not just for the accuracy of the text but for how it is delivered, and, to the extent possible, how it is received. It is rarely celebrated as "great writing," but the achievement of a "civic clarity" requires writers to take a step beyond accuracy. Using the tools of clarity, the writer strives for comprehensibility. That means helping readers understand the world. Armed with information, moved by powerful stories, engaged by sincere language, readers can act in their self-interest, even be moved to altruism.

Of course, honest writing requires the writer to avoid practices such as plagiarism and fabrication. Simply put, don't steal and don't lie. But "telling it like it is" requires avoiding more subtle failures. These include a lack of candor in describing the actions or language of a public figure who spreads disinformation that threatens the public health of a community or a president who tells big lies that inspire insurrection. Too often, public writers repeat the lies in their reporting without fact-checking. Or they feel a need to "balance" a responsible point of view with a distorted one. Such false balance reveals the limits of neutrality as a strategic practice.

I offer *Tell It Like It Is* as an antidote to the poisonous idea that journalists and other public writers and communicators are enemies of the people. That smear undermines the foundational institutions of knowledge that make self-government and democratic life possible. The cynical lies that seek to decertify journalism have metastasized to include attacks on institutions of science and medicine, on the courts and investigative instruments of government, and on higher education in almost any discipline.

Societies work best when these institutions exist in a network of interdependence and creative tension. To do that they must have a set of facts they can agree upon — or have honest arguments about. What are the practical consequences if a state makes most abortions illegal? What actions should a seaside community — like mine — take against the effects of climate change? When is it safe for me not to wear a medical mask? Why were parents and children of migrants separated at the border?

The answers to such questions are central to life, liberty, and the pursuit of happiness, if those ideals have any meaning at all. Journalism is just one profession responsible for helping us think through these questions in the public interest. But while journalists are necessary to the task, they are insufficient. We need many more public writers from other disciplines and professions: from education and the law, from business interests and nonprofits, from epidemiologists to social scientists, from academic poets to hip-hop artists. The more diverse the voices, the healthier our public discourse.

I would love to imagine that this book will be just one document leading to a renaissance of news and public information. This requires a rededication to plain language as a means and civic clarity as an end, to responsible storytelling as a way to get the public to pay attention, and to a clearer understanding of when a report should be neutral and when the engaged reporter needs to find a distance from neutrality. As I write this, there is an algae bloom called red tide polluting the Gulf of Mexico and Tampa Bay, killing countless fish and wildlife, filling the air with foul-smelling toxins that burn the eyes. It threatens the health, economy, and very essence of what it means to live in West Florida. What will we do about it? Who can help? What can we learn so we can lessen its effects now and over time? Journalists are working hard on the story. But so are scientists, public health experts, environmentalists, and officials at every level of government. Thank you, public writers. Keep it up. We need you. You are champions of the public good, of a healthy community, of what has become a fragile democracy. My future, our future, is in your hands. The hands holding a notebook and pencil. The hands moving across the keyboard. The hands holding this book.

Part I

Civic Clarity

Most of the writers I have worked with over the last half century have longed to be powerful storytellers, not just better explainers. That reveals why narrative writers get so much of the juice. They have more status. Their stories get better play. They win the more glamorous awards.

But literary grace has an equal partner in the work of public writing. I call it "civic clarity."

To balance the scales in the hearts and minds of writers, I have spent my career studying the best practices of the most influential public scribes. I read their prose as closely as if it were poetry, coming to understand how rhetorical moves and elements of news judgment combine to make things clear in the public interest.

The first twenty-four chapters of *Tell It Like It Is* share those moves as strategies you can use, as tools you can put on your workbench. We begin with the power that comes with identifying as a public writer and with imagining your readers not as customers but as members of a community who are trying to make sense of the world.

Public writers face dangers and temptations. We don't know enough. Or we know too much and forget what readers do not yet know. We learn the jargon from experts and veer from plain language. In frustration, we pack tough information and numbers into dense paragraphs. But we have tools to clear the clutter and smooth over the rough patches. And we have countless good examples, from a wide variety of writers, to inspire us to perfect our craft as writers.

1

Embrace the role of public writer.

A phrase I use a lot in this book—"public writers"—deserves careful attention. Who is a public writer? What does a public writer do? Where can we find public writers? When do public writers step forward in the public interest? Why should I think of myself as a public writer? If I want to be a public writer, how should I proceed? OK, I'm playing with questions that have been at the heart of the reporting process since the invention of the telegraph and the wire services, summed up as *who*, *what*, *where*, *when*, *why*, and *how*.

Four decades of my life have been devoted to the care and nurturing of writers, editors, and other workers who identify as journalists. They are the archetypal public writers, and their best work—their mission and method—constitutes the substance of this book. But it is well known that the enterprise of journalism is under great pressure. The business model of journalism has been depleted during the digital age. Thousands of journalists have left the business. Newspapers have disappeared, shrunk, or lost their news resources. Political partisans have worked to decertify the press, to cast doubt upon its credibility, even to call journalists enemies of the people.

Even if journalism were healthier, more profitable, and more energized, there still would not be enough reporters and editors with what it takes to create good governance and healthy communities. That's why we need more public writers than journalism can provide, more communicators helping to support responsible institutions, more writers — of every age and background — working in the public interest. More writers like you.

Many reporters and editors have left downsized news organizations. Many have joined the ranks of public writers. They now represent hospitals, universities, governments, airports, businesses, nonprofits, and other key institutions, doing their part to support the public interest. Their job is not to provide cover for higher-ups when things go bad. Quite the opposite. Their primary job is truth-telling for the common good.

If you are holding this book, chances are you are a public writer or aspire to be one. But who is a public writer? Isn't anyone who publishes anything a public writer? After all, the word *publish* holds the idea of the public inside it. By my definition, a public writer is any scribe who seeks a broad and diverse audience for stories or information in the public interest.

Public writers are champions of the common good. They make words like *democracy*, *self-government*, *public safety*, *social justice*, and *public health* come to life. When public writers do their job well, we all benefit. We learn more as citizens or members of a community and can take better actions. We vote. We help clean up a public park. We care about the education of children.

HIGHLIGHTS

- Wear the title *public writer* as a badge of honor.
- Pay attention to the news, even from information sources that you distrust.
- Use your writing craft with a sense of mission and purpose, focused on the common good.
- Before you write, jot down some notes about what you are trying to accomplish—e.g., "My friend just got a concussion falling off a motorized scooter while riding down Main Street without a helmet. I want to remind riders of the dangers."
- Sharpen your skepticism without falling into the pit of cynicism. Especially in dark times, shine a light on the hopeful and uplifting.

2

Study good public writing — wherever you find it.

In shaping my opinions about public writing, I have leaned on the work of reading and writing scholar Louise Rosenblatt, who spent most of her hundred years making people smarter. Her key insight went something like this: At times the writer wants the reader to notice the crafty work of the writer; and at times that is the last thing the writer wants.

The message in a text may be so important that the writer wants the reader to see it with no distractions about how smart the writer is or how the work was created. George Orwell offered this simile: "Good writing is like a window pane." We look through a window without noticing the pane — or the pain it took to achieve such clarity.

As a formative example, Rosenblatt offered the text on

the label of a poison bottle. If we drink from that bottle—for whatever reason—the antidote on the label may save our lives. The last thing the poisoned reader needs is a nice metaphor, or a clever turn of phrase. The reader needs language they can use—right now. The writer who created the clear message on that label has earned the title of "public writer." Few will understand the skill it took to create it.

It was Rosenblatt's distinction that came to mind as I administered to my wife in January of 2022 a COVID-19 antigen self-test "for infection detection." Hmm. That rhyme on the box is kind of clever, but I am more interested in the text that offered directions on how to prepare and deliver the test. My wife was recovering from the effects of chemotherapy for breast cancer, and she had a cold—or was it something more, such as COVID-19?

We acquired a product called BinaxNOW, produced by Abbott. At the time, it was considered among the more reliable self-tests. Early in the pandemic, we were tested twice at drive-through clinics, where we were told what to do every step of the way. This test would be different. It would take place in our kitchen. I would administer it, based on a set of directions with small illustrations. I read the directions on a four-page foldout. I read them a second time. Then I administered the test to Karen, following the nine steps described in the brochure.

After the test showed no evidence of COVID, I turned my attention back to the directions. Having experienced countless poorly written and organized directions attached to a variety of products, from children's toys to adult electronics, I was most impressed by what these writers had created to guide me through the process. I doubt that anyone would consider the directions "good writing." But that is how I saw it, and here is what I noticed.

1. The structure of the direction sheet was coherent. That is, the big parts fit together. They proceeded, of course, in chronological order: Do this, do this, do that. Stop! Did you do that? Big parts are labeled, white type over a black band:
    A. Prepare for the Test
    B. Collect Nasal Sample
    C. Perform the Test
2. It is often said that if readers can perceive the global structure of a piece early on (say, problem and solution), they are more likely to comprehend and remember.
3. Under those categories are steps to follow, a total of nine. Slowing down a complicated process, breaking it into practical steps, is a sure path to learning.
4. The layout offers lots of white space, sending the message that the directions will be easy to follow. I argue that white space is a form of punctuation, guiding lights that reveal the parts. To change the metaphor, white space also ventilates the page and releases the pressure of concentration, leading to a more inviting response from the user.
5. Words—not many—appear on the left, with clear illustrations on the right. The marriage of words and images—or WED: writing, editing, and design—creates a binary structure in which two disciplines of expression harmonize and reinforce each other.

6. Typography supports the message, from regular typeface to a few boldface words, strips of white type on black background, even red type for crucial cautions.

These elements of craft should illustrate how important it is for the writer to collaborate with designers, copy editors, illustrators, and others so that words find the most effective way to deliver an important message.

As for the language itself, let's examine a sample, the fifth step of nine:

> **Swab both nostrils carefully as shown.**
> Insert the entire soft tip of the swab in a nostril (usually ½ to ¾ of an inch).
> You do not need to go deeper.
> Using medium pressure, rub the swab against all of the inside walls of your nostril.
> Make at least **5 big circles.**
> **Do not** just spin the swab.
> Each nostril must be swabbed for about **15 seconds**.
> Using the same swab, repeat step 5 in your other nostril.

Let's do the math: seventy-eight words in short paragraphs, fifty-three words of one syllable. Most of the verbs are imperative; that is, they tell the reader what to do. That might create a voice that is too bossy for some, but it is the one we need at this instant. An expert teaches me how to proceed with a lot on the line.

Verbs include *swab, insert, rub, make, repeat.*

Think, for a moment, of the implications of getting

something wrong. The key is that the directions are a document that was created by writers and scientists who had a specific audience and a specific mission in mind. They have achieved civic clarity in the public interest. They are public writers.

It is helpful here to note that Abbott does not always express itself with such clarity. True, its website contains many clearly written reports in support of its products and services. But also included near the bottom of the site is a statement in smaller type labeled IMPORTANT SAFETY INFORMATION.

> The BinaxNOW™ COVID-19 Antigen Self Test is a lateral flow immunoassay intended for the qualitative detection of nucleocapsid protein antigen from SARS-CoV-2 from individuals with or without symptoms or other epidemiological reasons to suspect COVID-19 infection when tested twice over three days with at least 36 hours between tests.

This forty-nine-word sentence, compared to the language in the test directions, lacks the feel of public writing. I am not the intended audience. It has been produced for a different language club or "discourse community," the technical medical team and the legal team that build protection for the company against legal action. Maybe we should call it "small-print writing," the kind most people ignore when they are agreeing to the terms of a new digital service or legal contract. If certain texts require a degree of technical language, so be it, as long as the set of directions on how to take or administer a test are as clear as the set that guided me through the testing process.

There will be many more examples in this book of effective public writing, of writers using their craft to achieve civic clarity in the public interest. I offer this one first to send a clear message: In some ways, the anonymous authors of these directions are as important a group of public writers as the investigative team whose work appears on the front page of the *New York Times*. They may not know it, but they are all members of the same club.

HIGHLIGHTS

• In his book *On Writing*, Stephen King encourages writers to read bad writing so they can learn to avoid it. I work the other side of the street. Develop a keen sense of the kind of good public writing you would like to accomplish. Begin this process by collecting and then studying examples that work for you.

• When you are trying to describe something in the public interest, remember that every process has parts. To inspire action, you can turn those parts into steps.

• Here's a party game for public writers: Each person writes down an explanation of a common practice: making a peanut butter and jelly sandwich, pouring beer into a glass, eating an Oreo cookie. It's fun, and you can learn from the steps you leave out.

• Think of a time you gave or were given bad directions. What were the consequences?

3

Ask yourself these questions to achieve civic clarity.

Now that I have given you a taste of what civic clarity looks like in the directions of an at-home COVID test, I am going to share the techniques I believe all good public writers use. These strategies are well tested. I have shared them not just in newsrooms and university classrooms, but in organizations of all kinds with professionals who want to improve their writing in the public interest. These include the World Bank, IBM, HHS, NOAA, Disney, AAA, Microsoft, and the United Nations, just to name the most prominent. "We write about so many important and complex things," goes a common question, "but how do we make them clear and interesting?"

Questions are important to public writers, as we shall

see throughout this book. Some of the best questions are the ones writers ask themselves while they are planning or working on a text. I often ask myself questions about the purpose of my story, the kind of tone I want to set, what I hope readers will take away at the end. What follows, then, is a list of the most important questions public writers ask themselves when they are trying to achieve civic clarity. This list will give you a sense of the full landscape of writing strategies. In subsequent chapters, we'll dig into individual tools and offer telling examples. Get ready, writers. Open your toolbox.

1. How would I explain this to someone I know who is *not* an expert?
2. What have I learned about my technical topic that I now have to unlearn to avoid the temptation to start my text with what I know, rather than with what my readers *do not yet know*?
3. Where are the points of greatest complexity so that I can slow down the pace of information there?
4. Have I used shorter words, sentences, and paragraphs at the points of greatest complexity?
5. Which are the necessary numbers? Which ones are unnecessary and can be omitted?
6. Is there heavy cargo — technical data, statistics, etc. — that can be lifted from the text and placed in an illustration, an informational graphic, or a list?
7. Is there jargon, technical language from experts? What jargon can be avoided? Which terms need to be translated?

8. Do I need to find an expert who can explain things in plain English and who can be quoted without sacrificing technical accuracy?
9. Can I say with certainty that I have found my *focus* — the one key piece of knowledge I want to impart? If so, do all elements of the report support it?
10. Can I discuss a microcosm or small world that represents a larger reality: an intensive care unit rather than a whole hospital complex, a kindergarten classroom rather than an entire elementary school?
11. Is there a scene I can observe directly that would allow me to create a telling experience for my readers?
12. If I am writing about a policy, have I explored its impact and the effect a change might have on key stakeholders?
13. Can I explain something by focusing on the experience of one human being? A small group?
14. Are my sources diverse enough so that I can reveal all of the key stakeholders and several points of view?
15. What story elements — character profiles, dialogues, scenes, anecdotes — offer context for the information in my report?
16. If I were to give my readers a pop quiz on my story, would they be able to pass the test based on the information I have provided?
17. Is my story so clear that a reader could pass along the most important information to another person?
18. Can an analogy help me take an unfamiliar or complex concept and make it familiar?

19. Is there useless information I can delete from my report, so that readers are left with only the most useful?
20. Even though my work is clear, have I made it interesting enough so that readers will care?

HIGHLIGHTS

- This is the kind of list you might want to share with other public writers and editors, with students and teachers.
- Keep a copy close by so you can coach yourself through the challenges of achieving civic clarity.
- Put the list aside, and make another list of the kinds of questions you ask yourself at different stages of the writing process.

4

Slow down the pace of information, especially at points of complexity.

A child calls a parent on the phone and blurts out that they are in trouble, talking at the speed of sound. What does the parent say? "Slow down, honey, slow down. Now tell me what happened." The great writing teacher Don Murray taught me this lesson, and I have passed it along to countless writers: "Use shorter words, shorter sentences, and shorter paragraphs at the points of greatest complexity."

I borrow my most reliable illustration from my book *Writing Tools*. Here is a single sentence from an old editorial about state government. It is titled "Curb State Mandates."

> To avert the all-too-common enactment of requirements without regard for their local cost and tax impact, however,

> the commission recommends that statewide interest should be clearly identified on any proposed mandates, and that the state should partially reimburse local governments for some state-imposed mandates and fully for those involving employee compensations, working conditions and pensions.

The writer of this sentence is working hard, but not hard enough. The writer suffers from what Steven Pinker calls the "curse of knowledge." He has forgotten what he did not know. And now he knows so much, he makes the mistake of thinking the reader can keep up.

So how would you slow down the pace of "Curb State Mandates"? Here is my best try:

> The state of New York often passes laws telling local governments what to do. These laws have a name. They are called "state mandates." On many occasions, these laws improve life for everyone in the state. But they come with a cost. Too often, the state doesn't consider the cost to local governments, or how much money taxpayers will have to shell out. So we have an idea. The state should pay back local governments for some of these so-called mandates.

The differences in these passages are worth measuring. The original writer gives us one sentence. I give the reader eight. The original writer gives us fifty-five words, while I deliver eighty words in about the same amount of space, including fifty-nine one-syllable words. My words and sentences are shorter. The passage is clearer.

To the point, the pace of my version is slower.

Since it's easier to read, why don't I say the pace is faster? In a sense, yes, it feels faster because the path is smoother. But a sentence is a sentence. There is a period at the end. The Brits call the period a "full stop," and that's what it is, a stop sign.

The pace of longer sentences—well written ones, anyway—is fast because we are speeding along toward the period that completes the thought. A series of shorter sentences—with lots of stop signs—offers a slower pace, allowing readers more time to grasp a piece of information and then use that piece to get ready for the next sentence.

This is so important I want to repeat it: Too often, the reader gets sprayed with long, complicated sentences and just can't keep up. Think of the period as a stop sign. The more stop signs, the slower the pace, which is good if you are trying to make something clear.

Let's see how this might apply to coverage of a public health crisis. I found this brief description at cnn.com:

> The coronavirus is actually not one type of virus; it is a large family of viruses that also includes SARS and other minor to major respiratory illnesses. Coronaviruses can be spread between animals and people, as we have seen with this current strain. The term "corona," which is from a Latin root meaning crown or ring of light, refers to the shape of the virus under a microscope.

This feels like the right pace for helping readers learn. No need to resort to Dick and Jane sentences. Let's count the number of words in each sentence: 27-16-25. The pace is fairly easy, and the variation of sentence length gives the reader an agreeable rhythm.

That said, consider the effect of slowing down the pace even more:

> The coronavirus is actually not one type of virus. It is a large family of viruses. That family includes SARS and other minor to major respiratory illnesses, ones that affect your breathing. Coronaviruses can be spread between animals and people. That's what happened with this current strain. The term "corona" comes from a Latin root meaning crown or ring of light. It refers to the shape of the virus under the microscope.

You can decide if that's clearer. The word count is 9-7-16-8-7-14-11. I have revised three sentences into seven. Perhaps defining "respiratory illnesses" is a step too far. Reading the two passages again, I believe that mine is a little more comprehensible. There is still variety in length, but with a slower pace. That slower pace is created by those seven periods — seven stop signs.

This next example shaped my thinking about pace when I first read it years ago:

> When the price of sugar was plummeting last year, the federal government tried to help.
>
> Things didn't work out as hoped.
>
> What emerged is a complex struggle involving an interplay of governments, sugar producers, Third World

> economies, corn farmers and two grain milling giants based in Decatur.
>
> At stake are the price of sugar, the marketability of corn and the future of high-fructose corn syrup.

That passage may have been written decades ago by Jim Ludwick, an agricultural business writer in Illinois, but it continues to impress me with the way the writer shows concern for readers by easing them into what is going to be a complicated subject. Notice also the white space created by the decision to keep the paragraphs short.

HIGHLIGHTS

- Read your sentence aloud to see if you can follow it.
- If not, you may want to slow down the pace of information.
- This may require shorter words, sentences, and paragraphs.
- Think of the period as a stop sign.

5

Imagine writing for a single curious reader.

When you are ready to sit at the keyboard and write, you may already know too much. In other words, you forget that just a while ago you were a curious learner. Don't write down to the audience, but imagine how you would begin to explain your topic to a single person in a congenial chat.

The goal is to envision a general audience. A writer's sense of audience controls their voice. If I imagine and write for an audience of specialists, my language may seem technical and convoluted to the nonspecialist. These questions to a source might help: "Tell me in your own words what the issue is about." "Can we find a way to simplify this?" "Let's start from the beginning. What exactly is a pandemic?"

Many readers come to the same story looking for

different things. It can help the public writer to imagine writing for a single human being, and a familiar one at that. When you tell your story to a single person, your voice changes and your language becomes simpler and more direct. The editor can often play the role of this friend. One editor I know asks his writers to write him memos before they try to execute difficult stories. "When they put my name, Dear Fred, at the top of the page, it encourages them to write in plain conversational English."

Writing, of course, is not the same as talking. But there are many times when public writers want to create the illusion of conversation. When I listen to a public radio program, I can hear the actual voice of the writer. When I go to the website, I can "hear" that same voice when I read a text from the screen. Writers often talk about wanting to achieve an authentic voice. In most cases—except for broadcast reports, audiobooks, and podcasts—no writer is speaking aloud. The text is on a page or screen. But you can create the illusion of one person speaking to another. The most powerful tool for achieving this is addressing the reader directly as "you."

Also, when it comes to achieving civic clarity, you cannot overuse the question-and-answer format. Intelligent Q&As are appearing across media platforms, with questions coming from journalists and other members of the public. A question from a civilian has a way of getting experts to explain things in the language of the common person, at an easy pace. If the pace of information comes too quickly, the questioner can interrupt to slow the expert down. "Thanks for helping me understand cryptocurrency, sir, but you keep using this term 'blockchain' as a reason I can feel secure about my investment. Can you please explain how that works?"

HIGHLIGHTS

- If you could imagine writing for a single curious reader, who would that reader be?
- You can actually rehearse a story by having a conversation on a difficult subject with a friend or colleague.
- When you read your writing aloud, be aware of any language you use that is outside your conversational vocabulary. Use it if you need it, but is there a way to translate it?
- *You* is a powerful pronoun, one that sparks a sense of conversation. Just remember that in English we have two meanings for it. In the singular, *you* suggests one other person, but in the plural a group. You can write for one even though it will be read by many.

6

Avoid jargon — or translate it.

All of us are multilingual, which is to say that we belong to lots of different language clubs. My grandfather was Italian. My grandmother was Jewish. I have a degree in English literature. I play in a rock band. I coached girls' soccer. Each of those experiences has taught me to communicate in a different dialect. When I report on a technical subject, I have to learn a specialized language. But readers are out of the loop and will not understand jargon unless I teach it to them.

Wars, environmental disasters, hurricanes, recessions, and pandemics all generate countless technical terms. They come at us so quickly, we often let them fly by us as news consumers. For example, before I wrote this chapter, I could not tell you the difference between a coronavirus and COVID-19. Hmm, why were some reporters and specialists using one of those terms rather than the other? In a CNN glossary of related terms, we get this:

> COVID-19 is the specific illness related to the current epidemic. The acronym, provided by the World Health Organization, stands for "coronavirus disease 2019," referring to the year the virus was first detected. The name of the virus is SARS-CoV-2.

It may take a new public writer, covering city hall, a month or more to learn the acronymic alphabet soup of municipal government. Suddenly the writer feels comfortable sneaking technical words into stories without explanation. A problem arises when the writer's language is contaminated by his contact with specialists. Unless the writer translates "capitalization," or "amortization," or "depreciation," many readers will be left in the dark.

According to Glynn Mapes, a former Page One editor of the *Wall Street Journal*, that paper once defined *gross domestic product* ("the total market value of the output of goods and services in the nation") each time the term was introduced in a story. Editors at the paper kept a "recipe book" for quick and easy translations of technical terms. The *Journal*'s zeal for translating jargon once extended to defining *batting average* in a story about Ted Williams, the last hitter in baseball to hit more than .400 over a full season.

An example in the news caught my eye this morning.

Two professors of economics did their best to explain the Bitcoin "bubble," a recent investment crash related to how digital investors use "cryptocurrencies." The professors were shooting for civic clarity, but at times missed their target.

A single paragraph will reveal the problem:

> Today, the cryptocurrency universe is predominantly driven by speculators. They are, perhaps unknowingly, the angel investors in new crypto business models providing liquidity for crypto innovation. They are paving the way for new protocols (multi-signature, for example), new ecosystems (such as NFT marketplaces), new techniques (zero-knowledge proofs), and new payment networks.

Look inside those three sets of parentheses and you will find jargon that leaves me behind. I could look up *NFT (non-fungible token),* of course, and I did, but it feels like heavy lifting rather than an expansion of my mind as a reader, investor, and citizen. I need a glossary!

HIGHLIGHTS

- Technical language is fine if you are speaking to a specialized group and have learned, to borrow a phrase from T. S. Eliot, the "dialect of the tribe."
- Such language, called jargon and often ridiculed as gobbledygook, can have a bad purpose: to keep insiders in and outsiders out. Translating jargon, letting readers in on a

secret language, can have a democratizing effect on public discourse.

- Remember that you can avoid jargon and use plain language, or you can use the jargon and teach its meaning to readers.

7

Use as few numbers as will get the job done.

I learned this from *Wall Street Journal* writer and editor Bill Blundell, who became an influential writing coach: "My goal," he told me, "is to write a story without a single number. If I can't do that, then it is to write a story with only *one* really important number." Never clot a bunch of numbers in a single paragraph or, worse, three paragraphs. Readers don't learn that way. Numbers can be numbing. They turn off most readers, especially when numbers are packed into paragraphs or when they bump and collide:

> A proposed elimination of the 2 percent property tax rollback will immediately add $25 to each $1,000 in property taxes paid by middle- and upper-income taxpayers.

> In addition, the state is freezing its contribution to the 10 percent property tax rollback, which has been used as a tool to allow homeowners to keep pace with inflated property values.

This paragraph is not particularly offensive, but I am still trying to get my head around the idea of a contribution to a rollback. A series of such paragraphs is likely to block comprehension and send the frustrated reader elsewhere.

There are lots of confusing numbers coming from government officials and scientists. By reputation, public writers are more literate than they are numerate. When you are using numbers in a story, it is wise to triple-check. And have a reliable source with whom you can test your accuracy.

HIGHLIGHTS

- Numbers should be handled carefully in a story. Only the most important numbers should be used, and they should be explained in context.
- Ask yourself: Which number will really tell our readers what's happening?
- That big area of land is just an abstract number. Can we compare it to an area our readers will recognize?
- Those numbers make my head swim. What else costs that much?
- Can we get some help in turning those numbers into an easy-to-read informational graphic?

8

Lift the heavy cargo out of the text and put it in a chart or graphic.

I learned this from the world's best news and information designer, Mario Garcia. One way to handle numbers — or other technical information — is to deliver it in a visual way. Some things, like travel directions, are difficult to deliver in a text. A locator map — or Google map — may be better. But remember this: Just because it exists in a graphic does not mean it will be easy to understand. I have seen complex and incomprehensible stories turned into complex and incomprehensible graphics.

One of the key phrases to come out of the pandemic story is "flattening the curve." That phrase was everywhere — and it was crucial. Do you know what it means? I think I do, but I'm not sure I could explain it to my readers. I am a public writer, not a math teacher. *Flattening the curve* and *exponential* are math terms, far beyond the comprehension of the average reader.

Here is the best explanation I have seen in a text from an article in *The Nation*:

> Preventing a health care system from being overwhelmed requires a society to do two things: "flatten the curve"—that is, slow the rate of infection so there aren't too many cases that need hospitalization at one time—and "raise the line"—that is, boost the hospital system's capacity to treat large numbers of patients.

That is good public writing.

Informational graphics have reached new levels of excellence in all media platforms. Data visualization is evolving as its own explanatory discipline. A writer's ability to explain complex issues in words and then illustrate them in pictures provides valuable reinforcement for the reader or viewer. The writer should be on the lookout for important information that might be communicated effectively in a chart, graph, picture, illustration, or even animation.

Too often, organizations get divided up into creative silos. The writers are on one floor, the designers on another, the tech people hidden in a cloud. I cannot design a page. I am not literate in computer code. But because I have listened to my colleagues, and asked questions, and observed their best practices, I can now speak their language "without an accent." Together, we get our best work done.

HIGHLIGHTS

- A public writer may want to learn simple ways to illustrate a story, using simple visual elements.
- You need not be an expert in graphics and illustration, but you need to learn enough about those disciplines so that you can speak about them "without an accent."
- When you know your work will benefit from visual elements, send up a flare early in the process. Your colleagues need time and collaboration to produce their best work.

9

Reveal how the reader can use the information.

Imagine a story where a city is applying for a grant to build a plant to recycle sewage water. "They are going to do what?" asked the city editor. "Will we be drinking piss in this town?" The reporter set him straight: "No, Mike, you don't drink it. But you can water your lawn with it. And firefighters can put out fires with it. And it will save taxpayers a lot of money, especially during droughts."

I learned from my first city editor, Mike Foley, to always keep in mind the impact of public policy on ordinary citizens. He taught a generation of Florida journalists, including me, to avoid writing leads that read "They held a meeting Thursday." He was one of those great editors who wanted city hall reporters to cover more city and less hall. Too many stories fail to answer the reader's most challenging question: "So what?" The writer and helpful editor can ask it first.

One of the main challenges for public writers involves not just making important topics clear but making them interesting so that readers will pay attention and care. When I arrived in a newsroom for the first time in 1977, there was an undeclared consensus that certain kinds of reports defied the attempts of the most ambitious public writers to make them interesting. Near the top of the list was any story about a budget, especially one embedded in a bureaucratic process: the school board budget, the transportation budget, the city council budget.

The source of the problem is not in the content itself; it is not that a budget process is inherently uninteresting. It is that the writer might not be curious enough or enterprising enough to uncover the interesting elements in hibernation. A public writer cannot fake being interested.

People remember exactly where they were on significant historical days, such as the day JFK was assassinated, the moment the *Challenger* exploded, or the attacks of 9/11. But me? I remember where I was the morning that I read the best city council budget story ever written. The date was Wednesday, August 21, 2002. I was sitting at the breakfast table eating my Cheerios and reading the *St. Petersburg Times.*

The story was stripped across the bottom of the local section with this thin headline cutting across four columns:

City has $548 million to spend: What do you want?

I'm guessing now that it was the question mark that caught my attention, along with the unusual appearance of the second person *you.*

Then came the lead in the form of a seven-paragraph introduction:

> ST. PETERSBURG — Do you live in St. Petersburg? Want to help spend $548 million?
>
> It's money you paid in taxes and fees to the government. You elected the city council to office, and as your representatives, they're ready to listen to your ideas on how to spend it.
>
> Mayor Rick Baker and his staff have figured out how *they'd* like to spend the money. At 7 p.m. Thursday, Baker will ask the city council to agree with him. And council members will talk about their ideas.
>
> You have the right to speak at the meeting, too. Each resident gets three minutes to tell the mayor and council members what he or she thinks.
>
> But why would you stand up?
>
> Because how the city spends its money affects lots of things you care about.
>
> It's the difference between whether the Walter Fuller Pool is open and heated in the winter or not. It determines whether there will be a new basketball court in North Shore Park. It determines whether the beloved volunteer coordinator at the Office on Aging for senior citizens gets laid off.

At this point the story jumps to an inside page where there are quotes from city council members about their willingness to listen to the public. The story then dedicates a few paragraphs each to three different budget issues: the Boyd Hill Nature Preserve, the Western St. Petersburg library plan, and parking meters.

Accompanying the story are three informational graphics, two on the section front, one inside. One highlights the three key budget issues on the table. Another is a bulleted list of ways to influence city spending, with an email address for council members, directions to the city council meeting, and advice if you plan to speak there: "Plan to wind up your comments before your three minutes expire, or you will be cut off."

The final graphic is a budget summary and explanation that helps the reader distinguish between two broad categories of city spending: operating spending and capital spending.

Wow, I thought. This was remarkable. Perhaps even groundbreaking. I then did something I rarely do with such stories: I read it to the end. And then, because I could not believe my eyes, I read it a second time. This was a story I had been waiting twenty years to read.

Since that moment, I have encountered many examples of reports written with clarity and the reader's interests in mind. But never a city budget story, and, most certainly, never a city budget "preview." It is as if this was the unwritable genre, an inscrutable algorithm for poetry majors.

Then one steamy summer day something happened in a tiny village on the west coast of Florida. A reporter named Bryan Gilmer was covering the St. Petersburg City Council. Hear what he has to say:

"The thought of advancing the St. Petersburg city budget hearing bored me," Gilmer wrote in response to my questions. "I was, in fact, dreading it. It seemed like we wrote the same thing every year. Then I thought, 'Readers must really hate these stories if I don't even enjoy doing them.'"

Salvation appeared to Bryan in the unlikely form of Howard Troxler, the crusading metro columnist for the *Times*, who happened to be a summer fill-in as editor on the metro desk. Gilmer explains:

> Howard and I are fishing buddies, so I felt liberated to tell him frankly how I felt. He said we should find a way to have some fun with the piece, maybe even turn it into a Metro centerpiece. So we started chatting.
>
> I told him it annoys me that stupid issues in the hundreds of thousands of dollars often dominate the deliberations over a budget of nearly half a billion dollars. Some of these are just red herrings; others are tiny appropriations that have well-organized lobbying efforts behind them. Large items—especially ones not changing much from what was spent last year—usually slide right through. The City Council generally assumes that huge changes won't be made year to year. And the public figures the decisions are already made and that they can't influence them.
>
> They're sort of right. At this point in the "budget process," the mayor and council have all but agreed what the budget will look like. Hearing from the public is mostly a formality required by state law. . . .
>
> But shouldn't regular folks genuinely drive this plan

to spend a half-billion dollars forcibly collected from them? I'd plowed through the whole proposed budget myself, of course, and had written some about what was proposed. But what about what wasn't in there?

We agreed to fashion a story around the truth: People should know that the city's money was their money and that they could tell their representatives what to do with it. Howard said to write it like a column, and that he'd rein me in if I went too far. Then Howard and I agreed on a couple of the items we would highlight, and he took the lead in working with the page designer to round up pictures. I wrote some snappy chatter to accompany those.

Newspapers often assume their readers know much more about how government works than they really do. And newspapers are really bad at interacting with their readers, especially compared with other media like Internet publications. Who says we can't just talk to them sometimes, especially to explain complicated stuff?

So I wrote this piece in the second person. I used short sentences to make it an easy read for the government novices we pulled in with the graphics. And due largely to my strong feelings about the issue, it ended up... conversational, but with a point of view and a certain urgency.

In the end, readers indicated that they loved Gilmer's approach to the story, and many more of them than usual showed up at the meeting to indicate how they would like to see the city spend their tax dollars.

HIGHLIGHTS

Embedded in Gilmer's explanation are the strategies of civic clarity:

- Show how issues or the workings of government matter to readers.
- Write with a sense of audience so citizens, armed with information, can take action.
- Frame your writing in a way that gives agency to readers, revealing ways that they can take productive steps in shaping their communities.

10

Quote people who can make things clearer than you can.

A common piece of writing advice is to "Get a good quote high in the story." The key word is not "high," but "good." If you are working on a technical story, something about the rate of inflation or problems with the supply chain, you will be interviewing experts, so be careful. Experts have a way of showing off their expertise by using jargon. You don't have to be impolite: Rather than asking, "Can you give it to me in plain English, Doc?" you can ask, "How would that work?" "Can you give me another example?" "Can you please repeat that? I want to make sure I've got it right."

Over the years of the COVID-19 pandemic, a few key figures emerged as special sources of information for their capacity to translate technical language for the public good.

Most notable, perhaps, has been Dr. Anthony Fauci, a public expert on epidemics going back to the early days of AIDS. For political reasons he has been criticized and even threatened by people who refuse to follow medical advice based upon the best available data. That data often changes conclusions about the best practices for public health. I followed Dr. Fauci as a reliable if not perfect source of information. His sober, clarifying, and sometimes comforting messages came out loud and clear. He is not alone, and that's a good thing. I can think of a dozen scientists (such as Dr. John Torres and Dr. Sanjay Gupta) whose public presentations have been clear, responsible, candid, and encouraging, even during the darkest moments of the pandemic. We owe them a debt of gratitude.

When my wife was diagnosed with breast cancer in 2015, I turned to every source of information I could find to learn how to become a good caregiver. One source was an excellent book titled *Radical: The Science, Culture, and History of Breast Cancer in America*, a personal and social history of the disease, written by Kate Pickert, a journalist and cancer survivor. I took notes, marked passages, and wrote in the margins. As a writer, I was often impressed by Pickert's decisions about whether to explain things herself or to quote a source. For example, it turns out that chemotherapy treatments tend to differ depending on whether you live on the East Coast or West Coast.

That odd fact was best delivered by well-respected oncologist Larry Norton, who used a musical analogy: "There was East Coast jazz and there was West Coast jazz," said Norton, "and there is East Coast oncology and West Coast oncology. They're very different in their approaches to the disease."

Pickert explains that the approaches are cultural, not scientific. Back to Norton: "The New Yorker will say, 'What's the very best thing for me?' And the person from California will say, 'What's the thing for me that's pretty good but is the least harmful?' "

It turns out that Pickert has found a colorful and insightful source, whom she also quotes as saying "If you're standing in a dark room and you hear a gunshot, the odds are that the bullet is not going to hit you, but does that mean you shouldn't duck? I'm an East Coast doctor. I duck."

HIGHLIGHTS

- In your research, write down or record more quotes than you think you can use.
- When you write down a good quote, mark it with a star so you can find it again.
- It helps to get a human voice high in your story, but only if the voice sounds human.
- During interviews, don't be afraid to politely ask a question more than once to elicit a clear answer.
- In general, don't begin or end a story with a quote, unless it's a doozy.

11

Introduce a human being early. Let that person speak.

One human is more memorable than tons of data. I saw a photograph of a young woman trying to visit her grandfather at an assisted living facility. Because of his vulnerability to the coronavirus, she could not visit him or take care of him. But they could both put their hands on either side of a sliding glass door, that glass an emblem of the agony of our social separation.

Writers who write regularly about fiscal policy often fail to escape the clichés of economic writing. Budgets are not expressed as human documents but graphs that look like pizzas or thermometers. Stories are filled with bottom lines, tightened belts, economic spirals, and chopping blocks.

These stories seem not about people at all. No wonder readers look away.

Good writers understand that readers are attracted to the presence of human beings in stories. These humans can be politicians or bureaucrats, or they can be beneficiaries or victims of public policy. I learned this years ago from writers such as John Gouch, who explained the circumstances of Black farmers in South Carolina by focusing on the life and words of a single farmer. In the *Anderson Independent-Mail*, Gouch wrote, "Furman Porter was 4 years old when he first walked behind a mule plowing up Anderson County's red clay." The story was about the business of farming. A writer who focuses on a human being, and follows that character throughout the story, helps readers understand a policy's true consequences.

On occasion that human voice can be in a dialogue with the writer. My former student Mónica Guzmán begins her book *I Never Thought of It That Way* in a politicized conversation with her parents, immigrants from Mexico who became American citizens:

> On the morning of Election Day 2020, I was driving east from Seattle to my parents' house in Redmond, Washington, wondering if I should turn around.
>
> About a week earlier, I'd asked my parents if I could watch the results of the presidential election from their house. Mom blinked over her plate of carnitas tacos from the food truck down the way. She looked at Dad, then back at me.
>
> "*Claro*, Moni," she said in Spanish. *Of course, Moni.*

Then her eyes held mine a moment, asking what I was silently asking myself: *But are you sure you want to?*

After all, I'm a liberal who voted for Joe Biden, and Mom and Dad are conservatives who voted enthusiastically — and twice, now — for Donald Trump.

If a writer chooses to focus on a single character to embody a larger issue, it helps to keep this distinction in mind: Is the character being chosen because that person is representative of a larger group, or because that person stands out as extraordinary? In the first case, the writer may want to emphasize the details the character shares with the group; in the second, those details may be held back to make way for the ways the character is special.

HIGHLIGHTS

- You will meet a lot of people in your research. Not all of them can be in your story. Select the most important person — or the most interesting.
- When selecting players for your story, ask yourself: "Who has the most at stake?"
- Let that person speak high in the story.
- Choose the person strategically, either as representing a group, or as standing apart.

12

Develop a chronology.

Everything has a history. Everyone has a history. Every process or project has a history. When writers write about events in chronological order, they invite readers to enter a story and stick with it. Readers understand the demands of chronology and know that when the timeline ends, they will have reached a heightened level of understanding. Now I know why that building burned down. Now I know why that museum purchased that painting. Now I know how French fries became one of the world's most popular fast foods.

"I always try to find a chronology," says Chris Welles, who over the decades has written some of the most complex business stories in American public writing. Welles may be writing about a marketing war between BIC and Gillette, or the collapse of a major government securities firm, or the criminal indictment of a famous entrepreneur, but in each case he finds a chronological path that readers can follow.

These opportunities for chronology are not always transparent. If the writer is working with a teacher or an editor, the scribe can be inspired by a series of good questions that unfreeze time in a story, often turning flat explanation into narrative action. You can ask these questions to yourself: "When did that happen?" "How did that come to be? "Who knows the history of that problem?" "Who has been working there the longest?"

HIGHLIGHTS

- Whether or not you are writing in chronological order, develop a timeline to sort things out.
- The stories you write will often focus on the now. You can illuminate the current moment by looking back in time.
- When you are writing about an elementary school, don't just interview the brand-new principal. Interview the cafeteria lady who has been working there for thirty years.

13

Cool off. Set aside a draft to make sense of what you think you know.

Killer stories about complex issues often involve intense periods of research and learning for the writer. A cooling-off period gives the writer time to understand what they know, what they still must learn, and how best to communicate meaning to the readers.

Those of us who try to publish in the heat of the moment run serious risks. Attempting to explain complicated information, we get defensive about our long and unclear and complicated sentences. "Of course it's complicated," we yell to no one in particular. "The policy is complicated." This can be a mask for "I don't really understand it, so I'll fog over my uncertainty with cloudy prose."

Writing coach Donald Murray recommends that writers "schedule a ritualistic time for standing back" on such stories, saying:

> This should be a time when the writer puts all the notes and documents aside, stares out the window, sips a cup of coffee, and tries to think about what they have learned that day. It may be a good idea to attempt to put down, in a subject-verb-object sentence, the most important development of the day.

Letting a draft cool off for a while also helps writers improve their prose. The longer the cooling-off period, the better the writer can see their own work with a clear eye. When I reread a published story from months or years ago, I see things I wish I had changed, things that were invisible to me in the heat of a deadline. But you don't need a year. Sometimes all you need is a coffee break.

HIGHLIGHTS

- In the middle of difficult research, put your materials aside and think about what you learned today.
- Get away from the keyboard, desk, office, even if it's just for a while.
- Have a friendly chat with a friend or coworker to hear yourself speak about your story.
- After you have written a draft, step away, even for a moment, and return with fresh eyes for revision.

14

Eliminate unnecessary information.

The best way to deal with difficult information is to leave it out of the story. Too many stories contain too much information for the reader to digest. Readers may understand more if we give them less. The key to doing this responsibly is to make tough value judgments about the information we have collected. Testing for accuracy and factuality is the first task. But a text can be accurate and factual and still be difficult to grasp. You must decide which elements are truly the most interesting and most important. The result of such selectivity is a more precise, more readable story. If it turns out to be boring and difficult, at least it will be brief, boring, and difficult. Readers will be thankful writers did not waste their time.

Another important step is to unpack dense paragraphs.

A good teacher does not expect students to learn everything at once. Yet too much writing on tough subjects is of the "dense-pack" variety: information stuffed into tight, thick paragraphs and conveyed at a rate that takes our breath away. Consider this paragraph:

> The billing structure and data-gathering procedures are geared toward providing cost-based reimbursement to satisfy federal regulations under Medicare... which insures about 40 percent of Arizona's hospital patients.

I've tried and tried to translate this sentence, without success. My process was to try to break it into pieces of knowledge:

"40 percent of the hospital patients in Arizona are insured under Medicare."

"Medicare is a federal program."

"If you want to be reimbursed, you have to satisfy some federal regulations."

"Arizona hospitals seeking reimbursement pay special attention to the structure of their billing and to the way they gather data."

"If they do these things right, there is a better chance they will get reimbursed."

That's the best I can do. If you were to read my unpacked passage aloud, it would take you longer than reading the original dense sentence. To give you five sentences, I need five periods — the stop signs of punctuation. I give you room and time to learn.

When striving for clarity, it's crucial to cut the clutter,

especially at the top. For a story that is difficult or complex, the public writer must pay special attention to the lead, or beginning. If the lead is crammed with information or demonstrates to readers that the subject is beyond their interest and understanding, the reader will turn elsewhere:

> Efforts to improve housing for Buffalo neighborhoods will receive $5.6 million of the city's annual federal community development block grant money, according to the application to be submitted to the Common Council tomorrow.

The combination of numbers, jargon, and needless attribution dooms this lead. The writers can ask these questions: "How much money is $5.6 million? What will it accomplish?" "There are no people in the lead. Who are the key players? Who will benefit most?" "Explain this application process to me. Is this going to happen or not?" "What do readers really need to know about this?" Perhaps such questions would lead to something more like this:

> Some people in Buffalo think the city needs more and better housing for its citizens. They are trying to do something about it and are asking for help from the federal government. More than $5 million worth of help.

Difficult ideas can often be expressed in simple sentences. Simple sentences are usually short, clear, and easy to read. They contain one clause and one idea. A series of simple sentences also slows the pace for the reader. Each period is a stop sign. The reader has time to digest and assimilate information. It also helps to think of subjects and verbs as conjoined twins. The clearest sentences almost always keep subject and verb together near the beginning. When subjects and verbs in the main clause are separated, all kinds of mischief can occur.

When brevity and simplicity give way to complexity and opacity, the result can read like this:

> A 3.6-billion-dollar compromise budget was agreed to by House Senate Ways and Means Subcommittees yesterday that pares one billion dollars from the previous compromise budget of 4.6 billion dollars, of which 993 million dollars may be restored when it returns to the floor of the Senate next week.

"The more complicated the subject," taught writing coach Donald Murray, "the more important it is to break the subject down into digestible bites."

HIGHLIGHTS

- Cut clutter in a piece of writing wherever you can find it, but pay special attention to the top of the story.
- Eliminate weaker elements so the stronger ones stand out.
- It helps to keep subjects and verbs together near the beginning of a sentence.

15

Introduce new or difficult elements one at a time.

A tough story to read is the one that introduces twenty characters in a dozen paragraphs. The frustrated reader turns back again and again to keep things straight, or just gives up.

Help the reader by introducing one character or one concept at a time. When Chris Welles explained to the readers of the *Los Angeles Times* how accountants helped Orion Pictures launch its financial comeback, he had to explain "generally accepted accounting principles," known by the shorthand *GAAP*. That done, Welles was able to deal with each of the accounting techniques used at Orion. He introduced them slowly, one at a time: "Certainly the most unusual accounting strategy used by Orion was what is known as 'quasi-reorganization.'" Welles lets us into the secret of how it works. In this long, difficult story, he gives the reader a chance to relax, to think, to understand.

I recently discovered a book for children with the ambitious goal of explaining ideas from Charles Darwin's *On the Origin of Species*. Clear explanations accompany beautiful illustrations, inviting readers of all ages—including me—into a journey of understanding. I noticed a glossary at the end that includes these terms: *adaptation*, *ancestor*, *descendant*, *DNA*, *evolve*, *extinct*, *fossil*, *genes*, *genus*, *primates*, *sediment*, *species*, *variation*. I realized that I had encountered all of these technical terms in the text—but not all at once! Author and illustrator Sabina Radeva introduces them one at a time, in the best possible order for creating interest and leading to understanding.

Some medicines go down hard, and some concepts, issues, or procedures are so difficult that even careful and thoughtful writers cannot make them palatable for readers. That is as it should be. It would be dishonest to give readers a false sense of simplicity. That is why writers will, on occasion, inform readers that certain information will be rough going.

Business writer Chris Welles let his readers know what they are in for if they are to understand the complexities of "risk arbitrage":

> Until recently... risk arbitrage has been largely unknown beyond Wall Street and only vaguely appreciated even on Wall Street. One reason was arbitrage's image as a highly intricate, arcane, even mysterious art well beyond the ken of ordinary investors.

Such announcements sharpen the concentration level of readers. They gain tolerance for harder information. They express gratitude on being let in on an important secret.

HIGHLIGHTS

- Make a list of the most important technical terms or concepts you want your readers to learn.
- Divide them into two groups: more important and less important.
- Now choose the one that readers need to learn first.
- Try to explain that term without using any additional technical language.
- List the concepts in what you think is the best order.

16

Value repetition.

Teachers know the value of repetition. They adhere to the old strategy: "Tell them what you are going to say, say it, then tell them what you've said."

Editors of public writers tend to be suspicious of repetition. It takes up space. But why not repeat the key information to demonstrate its importance to the reader? The goal of public writers is to recognize the heart of a story and reinforce it in a headline, a blurb, a drop quote, and a caption.

"I try to teach reporters that if they have an important point they want to make, make it repetitiously but in different ways," editor Bill Blundell taught me at a Poynter Institute writing seminar. "Make it with a figure, make it with an anecdote, and then maybe wrap it up with a quote." Variation saves the repetition from looking like redundancy.

"You cannot be explicit enough in communication," preached John Robinson, a scholar of communication, to an audience of working journalists. "Leaving something between the lines and thinking the reader is going to get it is a very dangerous practice."

There are points in this book that I do not want to leave between the lines, points that are so important that I have repeated them in a variety of contexts: that public writers are champions of democracy, that they strive for an effect I call "civic clarity," that to make something clear they control the pace of information, that they pay attention to what is interesting and important, that they write reports and stories, that they will want to be neutral about many things, but not every thing. If you recognize some of those phrases, it is not because I have been carelessly redundant. It's because I have learned in fifty years of marriage that you can't say "I love you" too many times.

HIGHLIGHTS

- Do your best to find the focus of your story, the heart of it, what you most want readers to remember.
- Share that focus with colleagues who are working on the project with you.
- Use all your tools to impart that focus: the title, the lead, a caption, a statistic.
- Variation neutralizes redundancy.

17

Compile lists.

Public writers use the "laundry list," technically called the "bulleted list," to compile the most important information in a meaningful order. Investigative writers list their major findings high in the story. A city hall reporter lists the alternatives for financing a new baseball stadium. (I list ways to make hard facts easy reading!) Lists create order, or at least the sense of order. They demand that the writer convey information tightly. They invite the reader to choose the item they most care about. Lists also create white space and typographical structures that invite the reader's eye to move down the page or the screen.

HIGHLIGHTS

- In your research, you can list items in your notes as you learn them.
- In your writing, you can order the list, using handy methods from alphabetical to chronological to priority.
- Readers are most likely to recognize and remember the first item in a list, or the last. You can also place a key item right in the middle.
- The names of rescued dogs might be Moonlight, Ralph, Rex, Lucy, Olive, Lance, Goober, Dakota, Bubba, Brandy, and Casanova. Think of all the cool ways you could order those names.
- A fun and creative way to handle lists is to place each item on a card or a Post-it Note and then play with the order. Reading items aloud offers a possible rhythm to the list.

18

Apply these tests to see whether you have achieved civic clarity.

So you have embraced the role of the public writer. You are writing on a complex topic of public importance. You do your best, using a number of the strategies you have learned above. You have a sharp focus. You set a nice pace for the information. You translate the jargon. You emphasize the impact on real human beings. And so forth. How do you know, then, if you have been understood? The writer's hope is that the reader understands. It is my mission to make this clear for the reader. If the reader does not understand, I have not done enough. I promise to try harder next time.

Every text will be clear to the reader who knows enough. Researchers have demonstrated that prior knowledge is the most significant variable to comprehensibility.

The implications are staggering. It means that written work that is unclear, awkward, even clumsy may be understandable to an expert on your subject. So it makes sense for you to learn what you can about your audience before you make the key language choices for a text. My preference is to write for multiple audiences at the same time, a trick I learned from Shakespeare. The cheap "seats" at the Globe Theatre were near the stage. That's where the groundlings stood, and where, it is said, the swordplay and bawdy jokes were most appreciated. Up in the actual seats sat the aristocracy, who, I bet, liked the sex and violence, too, but were more prepared to appreciate the most dramatic poetry ever written.

I will say it again: public writers must write in a way that explains important and complex issues. Then, goes an idealistic theory, informed citizens can make the daily decisions that affect their lives. Will I vote for the council member who supported that tax? Will I shop there anymore? Will I send my child to public school? Will I sell my house? Should I save my money?

HIGHLIGHTS

Writers can apply these tests to their prose. If you can answer yes to these questions, you are already using the tools of clarity in your work.

- Is my writing clear enough that a reader could pass a quiz on the important information in the story?
- Is it relevant enough that a reader could pass along accurate information from the story to another person?

- If you asked the reader, "What's important in this story?" would the reader agree with the writer?
- After reading a story, does the reader have enough information that they can take specific action, such as attending that meeting or avoiding that intersection?

19

Read the public writing on the wall.

My hometown, St. Petersburg, Florida, is a city of museums. Imagine Museum and the Chihuly Collection at the Morean Arts Center display astonishing glass artworks; the Florida Holocaust Museum is a place that moves the mind and the heart; and the Salvador Dalí Museum, well, what can I say, it's surreal. The new kid on the block is the James Museum of Western & Wildlife Art.

The first texts I ran into when I entered the James Museum were two "Youth Activity Guides." I am not embarrassed to say that I learned a lot from the guide created for ages six and up. (Add sixty-eight years to that number six and you will know my current age.)

The three-page guide offers three lessons on how artists use shape, form, color, and line. Here is a taste:

> There are two kinds of shapes. Geometric shapes are precise and uniform, like circles, squares, and triangles. Organic shapes are freeform and irregular, like rocks, leaves, and clouds.

The creators of the guide leave lots of white space for easy reading and add useful illustrations for quicker learning. Even better are creative activities, beginning with the image of a red and yellow stagecoach: "Find this stagecoach in the Frontier Gallery. What shapes do you see? Design your own unique stagecoach. Try using geometric and organic shapes." That would be an ambitious project for a seven-year-old, not to mention a seventy-four-year-old.

The second guide is for ages eleven and up and introduces more challenging concepts, such as perspective:

> *Perspective* is used to create a sense of depth in a design. There are two types of perspective:
> *Non-linear perspective*: Position or overlap elements in a design to create depth. Elements placed higher on a canvas appear farther away. Elements that overlap in front of others appear closer.
> *Linear (one-point) perspective*: Parallel lines converge in a single vanishing point to give the illusion of depth.

Illustrations and diagrams are essential for learning. But let's not ignore the way that the authors translate the technical jargon of the visual arts for a multigenerational audience.

If you were to follow me through a museum gallery, you would be amused. While others stand back to take in the visual experience of art, my nose is pretty close to the accompanying text block. My style is to glance at the image, read the text, then stand back and enter into the picture.

Take for example, this text accompanying the painting *Bronco Break* by American artist Thomas Blackshear II:

> Oil on canvas
>
> After the Civil War (1861–1865) with few employment opportunities available to freed men of color, many found work as cowboys. The role did not provide an escape from racism, as Black cowboys often were given the toughest jobs, but they typically had greater autonomy than former enslaved people in other occupations.
>
> While their contributions to Western expansion were significant, Black cowboys have long been overlooked in the larger narrative of American history and portrayals in art and pop culture. Fortunately, dialogue around diversity in the West has spotlighted more African American perspectives in recent decades. Today's Black cowboys—and cowgirls—have continued family traditions of riding and roping for generations.

I am so impressed by this prose and by other such public texts. I recognize them all the time now in informational and presentational works such as guides about animals, stars, architecture, important places, and much more. In most examples, the author is not using the first person, yet the voice emerging from the text does seem helpful and conversational, imagining a reader who may have some questions.

This style of public discourse has been described by scholars Francis-Noël Thomas and Mark Turner as "classic." They argue that a passage in the classic style—delivered either orally or in print—has certain stylistic requirements, or, if not requirements, then benefits. Even though there is the feel of one side of a smart conversation, there is no sign of the first person or the second, which in other cases would signal a type of informality. The third person works best. The scholars insist that writing the classic way avoids digressions, side trips, even the transitions of print such as "as we mentioned earlier" or "looking into the future." Instead, the style is straightforward and confident, information delivered with an authority that doesn't seem bossy or pedantic.

HIGHLIGHTS

- Start paying more attention to public texts (or published ones) designed to inform and educate about things a curious person might want to know.
- Look for the presence (or absence) of the first or second person, paying special attention to texts in the third person that avoid *I* and *you*.
- Even if you are presenting information in the classic style—without using *you*—imagine an audience of curious people. Think of the questions they might ask you.
- As always, read your text aloud, even if it is not written for oral presentation. Read a draft to another person and ask how it sounds. Is it clear on first reading? Does it feel confident and authoritative?

20

To serve the largest audience, write within the first "circle of clarity."

It's easy to assert that good writing must be clear. But we know from the study of literature, say, or philosophy, that at times good writing is not clear, either by intent or effect. That doesn't mean that good writing should be opaque or hopelessly dense. It can mean that the writer is striving to grasp and communicate a difficult thought, one that demands more than average work on the part of the reader.

In my first college poetry class, I sat in wonder and confusion as our teacher recited the first lines of "The Windhover" by English poet—and Jesuit priest—Gerard Manley Hopkins:

> I caught this morning morning's minion, king-
> dom of daylight's dauphin, dapple-dawn-drawn Falcon...

I could catch the poem's beauty—a vision of a bird, its wings stretched out in the shape of a cross, its body buckling against the force of the wind. I have come to learn that this is the work of a gay priest and poet of the Victorian era, trying to reconcile religious and sexual ecstasy. No reason for that poem to have a transparent meaning. It deserves work on the part of the reader.

That leads me to questions on behalf of all public writers: When do we know that we have achieved "civic clarity"? What do the words "clear and comprehensible" mean in practical terms? These questions have a long history, going back centuries, reaching a plateau in the 1940s and '50s. Two authors in particular created readability studies, which tested "ease of reading" based upon algorithms that counted the average length of sentences and the average number of syllables per hundred words. Rudolf Flesch created the influential Flesch Test. Robert Gunning, who worked with many businesses, created the Fog Index. Both approaches had value and retain it, even though they were ridiculed by the likes of literary figures such as E. B. White. "Writing is an act of faith," wrote White, "not a trick of grammar." He referred to the readability tests as "calculating machines."

In one of several versions of his test, Flesch would drop an examined piece of writing into one of five boxes: fairly easy, standard, fairly difficult, difficult, and very difficult. Helpful, I think, but complicated when he attached those categories of reading to educational levels: sixth grade, eighth grade, some high school, high school or some college, and college. In other words, it would probably take a reader with a college education to comprehend a text that was "very difficult."

I know some eighth-graders capable of reading difficult texts, and some college grads who struggle with the basics.

Let me offer, tentatively, another way of judging the clarity of a text. We could certainly create, say, a spectrum, a scale of one to ten, in which "one" is muddy and incomprehensible and "ten" is crystal clear. And let's stipulate that one paragraph in a report might be cluttered and pointless, while another might lead you to a clear meaning.

As I looked at texts and evaluated their clarity, I wound up drawing four circles on a piece of paper, numbering them from 1 to 4.

Circle 1 was the biggest, containing the most readers. Circle 2 was smaller and Circle 3 even smaller. Circle 4 was the smallest of all, containing the fewest readers. Please stick with me.

Circle 1: The largest circle. Clear to most readers. In fact, writing that younger or less experienced readers can share with more experienced readers.

Circle 2: Not every reader can understand, but the common reader can, especially the reader who needs or wants to know.

Circle 3: Clear to the more informed reader and the reader who is willing to learn, but more challenging to the common reader.

Circle 4: Clear to a specialized audience that already possesses some technical knowledge—for instance, business reports for investors.

It's fair to say that every text is comprehensible to the reader who comes to it possessing enough prior knowledge. That means that there is a Circle 5 to infinity. Those circles, reaching fewer and fewer readers, can be counted only as specialized or technical writing, not public writing. A technical essay in a medical journal, for example, may be comprehensible only to other scientists and technicians. It may take a public writer to translate it.

By no means will I argue that texts beyond Circle 4 constitute bad or irresponsible writing. Take this example of a summary in a student paper written for a college biology class (from *A Short Guide to Writing About Biology* by Jan A. Pechenik):

> The tolerance of a Norwegian beetle (*Phyllodecta laticollis*) to freezing temperatures varied seasonally, in association with changes in the blood concentration of glycerol, amino acids, and total dissolved solute. However, the concentration of nucleating agents in the blood did not vary seasonally.

The audience for this writer is imagined as people who already understand its technical language. It would not take much to work the content into Circle 4. In its current state, it is not intended for a public audience.

In this view, a text in Circle 1 is most comprehensible to the greatest number of readers, but not every reader, of course. I don't mean Dick and Jane primer language. An eighty-year-old grandparent reading E. B. White's *Charlotte's Web* aloud to an eight-year-old grandchild could be an enthralling and entertaining experience for both of them.

When we get to a text at Circle 4, we are talking about

something that might be quite clear but only to a small group of readers with a specialized vocabulary within a particular discipline—from prison slang to the scientific notations of epidemiologists. Public writers should always begin with some sense of their intended audience, while leaving doors and windows open for the most eager and curious and determined learners.

To test this out, I explored a text from March 2021. It was written by a student named Aiden Segrest for the Lakewood High School news site in St. Petersburg, Florida. This school is walking distance from my house, the alma mater for my three daughters. Since the 1980s, Lakewood has been home to some excellent student journalists. Aiden's column is nine paragraphs long. Here is the headline: **COVID-19 doesn't just go away**. The sub-headline: "After having the Coronavirus, he realized it was a much different experience than he had thought."

He begins:

> In November, I tested positive for Coronavirus as did my close family. With COVID-19, you do not always feel under the weather, but when you do, it feels worse than the flu. For me I had three not so unique COVID symptoms.
>
> My first symptom was coughing, the most common symptom. It's not so nice. The coughing I felt when I had the virus reminded me of when I was a child and could not get rid of the croup cough.... This coughing was violent and came in fits, usually prompted by things like staying up later and talking too much as well as eating cold things.

> The second symptom I had was arguably the worst, a lack of taste or smell. At first, I didn't notice anything because the lack of those senses is much less apparent when they go away gradually. Even when I was over COVID for two and a half weeks, my sense of taste was not exactly strong, and my sense of smell was practically nonexistent. It's like breathing air in your room; you're used to all the smells and so you just breathe air rather than smell.
>
> The lack of taste was apparent when I bit into a burger with pickles and could not taste it. I just felt the texture as I bit into it....

Let me begin with an appreciation of what Aiden is doing. He is crafting a clear and cautionary tale, and he has a sharp sense of his audience: the students at Lakewood and their families. Aiden understands the invulnerabilities that many young people feel and offers a real experience of COVID by a young person, with this warning at the end: "I didn't even know I had COVID until my test came back. I thought it was just a cold. Thankfully, I take online school, so it wasn't much of an issue, but if you end up infecting your family, you may end up regretting it dearly."

Aiden makes an honest assumption about the practical knowledge of his readers. He assumes they know what COVID is, that he is writing during a pandemic, that students are working from home, that there is testing going on. There are still students—and adults, I fear—who may not know or care about that, and who may find parts of the column incomprehensible. That said, I am willing to place

Aiden's prose squarely in Circle 1, clear for the great majority of readers.

HIGHLIGHTS

Aiden Segrest was a sixteen-year-old high school sophomore when he wrote his column. Let's do a quick inventory of Aiden's rhetorical approach, some elements of his style that create civic clarity, and tools that should be on your workbench:

- Use sentences and paragraphs of reasonable length.
- Use common words, and many one-syllable words: "a lack of taste or smell."
- You can use some technical language (COVID, symptom, croup, congestion), but not too much, and in a context that makes it understandable.
- Analogies can be quick and simple: "It's like breathing air in your room."
- Move from the top of the ladder of language (lack of taste) and illustrate it at the bottom of the ladder where you can appeal to the senses: "I bit into a burger with pickles...."

21

Write for both those in the know, and those who want to know.

I have offered, more than once, the idea that what makes a text clear—or at least clearer—depends upon what the reader already knows. The capacity to comprehend is influenced but not determined by age and educational level. If I could find the best high school science students in Florida, I'm sure they would be able to understand certain texts about epidemiology that I cannot—even with my Ph.D. in medieval literature. (I may be ahead of them on stories about the bubonic plague!)

In my imagined circles of clarity, Circle 1 contains texts that can be understood by the greatest number of readers.

But what if I want or need to write for a smaller, more specialized audience? I might begin by studying the work of

New Yorker writer Sue Halpern, such as her article "Why COVID-19 Vaccines Aren't Yet Available to Everyone." This piece of public writing—or explanatory journalism, if you prefer—has a clear mission: to answer a question crucial to public health and safety, a question that has life-and-death consequences.

What may be clear or comprehensible to readers of *The New Yorker*—known for its sophisticated literature, nonfiction, and humor—may be lost on some members of the general public, even the ones now eager or desperate for vaccinations. Writing for Circle 1 may be insufficient to the task.

Let's look at her first paragraph:

> About a year ago, Chaz Calitri, the head of operations for sterile injectables at Pfizer, was at home in suburban Philadelphia, when he got a call from his bosses. The company was moving forward with an experimental COVID-19 vaccine. Calitri, a chemical engineer by training, was in charge of Pfizer's manufacturing site in Kalamazoo, Michigan, where the constituent parts of the vaccine would eventually be assembled before being shipped across the country. "At first, I was really excited," he told me. "And then, after I sat down on the couch and started thinking about it, I was horrified, because I knew that it was going to take the full force of everything we could throw at it."

In spite of technical language such as "sterile injectables," I would argue that this paragraph works as a way of easing the reader into a technical story. The common language of "he got a call from his bosses" triggers the action. An old maxim in the newsroom advises the writer to "get a good quote high in the story." Mission accomplished, as we can understand how a worker, a leader, can become excited by an important new job, and then terrified by it.

The length of paragraphs contributes to readability and comprehensibility. Magazine columns and book pages are wider than newspaper columns, which allows paragraphs to be longer. But I see no reason why that first paragraph need be 117 words long. Without more white space, easily created by additional paragraph breaks, the text will appear dense to the eyes of the reader. Why not give that great quote its own space? If you have something really good, let it breathe.

After Halpern sets the stage in her introduction, she offers this passage:

> When the President of the United States places an order for millions of doses of COVID-19 vaccine, they do not simply appear, like Amazon packages, two days later. [That is an effective opening to a new paragraph — with a great analogy attached.] For much of the past year, it has taken Pfizer a hundred and ten days to produce each vial of vaccine. The time line starts at the company's plant in Chesterfield, Missouri, outside St. Louis, which houses a cell bank of frozen *E. coli* bacteria. Scientists extract DNA from the *E. coli* cells to grow the template, called a plasmid, on which the vaccine's mRNA will be built. [I am getting worried now, not quite able to make sense or keep up with the science.] Once the plasmid is made, purified, and tested, the double-helix structure of the DNA has to

> be linearized—literally, made linear. [Happy for the translation, though a little hard to see the process.] The process takes about ten days, after which it goes through additional testing. "We're going twenty-four hours a day with three manufacturing shifts," Christine Smith, the Chesterfield-site leader told me. "And then there's another shift making all the buffers and media to grow the cells in and getting ready for the next day. It's a very regimented process. It's not like we can just open up a door to the room next door and start making it."

One test of a great level of civic clarity would be my ability to read this story and to pass on the information to another curious person. "Hey, TJ, this is the reason why the vaccines are not available to everyone. It's a darn complicated process. You just can't snap your fingers and ship it off." So yes, I can get that much. But a description, based on science, of how the process works remains beyond me.

Still, I rank this an excellent example of public writing, accessible not to everyone but to an important segment of rank-and-file citizens. I would place it in Circle 3 or 4.

HIGHLIGHTS

- Find out as much as you can about who your readers are and what they know.
- Shakespeare wrote for the groundlings and the aristocrats. Imagine writing for multiple audiences, where some members know a little and others know a lot.

- When you feel you have to use a technical term, translate it for the reader.
- When you can, introduce a likeable and knowledgeable expert who can help you explain.
- Find a cool entry point—like when a person receives a high-stakes phone call.

22

Look for the apt analogy.

To achieve a level of civic clarity requires basic skills, such as cutting words that do not work. The most effective public writers have mastered advanced skills, such as the formation of an apt analogy. It is a powerful but underutilized tool on the writer's workbench. A distant cousin of the metaphor and simile, the analogy is a gift from writer to reader. The writer takes something that might be difficult to understand and holds it up against something readers may already know about.

In America, this speaks to the popularity of the length of a football field. A muscled-up golfer drives a ball 380 yards, the length of almost four football fields. A huge oil tanker is 380 meters, or 1,247 feet, or 415 yards — yes, greater than the length of four football fields. The football field, like the distance to the moon and back, have become cliches of comparison. Good writers are capable of so much more.

How do we make sense of the enormity of more than one million dead from the pandemic? One way, of course, would be to return to the football field, or in this case one of the largest football stadiums in America. Certain college venues hold 100,000 fans, so the math is easy, though the reality unthinkable—that the dead could fill such stadiums ten times over. Such an analogy, I would argue, lacks decorum.

More artful and appropriate in terms of language and message is the simple analogy offered by Julie Bosman in a *New York Times* story: "More Americans have perished from COVID-19 than on the battlefields of World War I, World War II and the Vietnam War combined." While there are limits to the value of comparing a pandemic to a war, in this context the comparison has an appropriate and sobering effect.

Often an analogy works better in a graphic illustration rather than words, or in a marriage of words and pictures. A dazzling digital graphic in the *Washington Post*, created by Artur Galocha and Bonnie Berkowitz, offered three visual analogies for the human dimensions of the first half-million to have died from the disease.

To take a half-million people on a bus tour would require 9,804 buses, a caravan that would stretch almost 95 miles, the distance from New York to Philadelphia. To honor the names of the dead on a memorial, you would need blocks of marble eight times taller than ones that honor the 58,000 dead from the Vietnam War. If you buried the dead in a single cemetery, you would need one just as big as the one that now exists at Arlington. To account for a million Americans dead would mean that whole cities—San Francisco or Seattle—would be wiped out.

Such remarkable images of the enormity of loss can never replace the particular loss experienced by a particular family suffering the absence of a particular loved one, whose full life deserves a narrative of appreciation, like the ones created by the *New York Times* to honor those who were killed by terrorist attacks on September 11, 2001.

Discovery of the apt analogy requires the writer to master the technical material. While simple comparisons can enrich a text, more sophisticated examples can transform the experience of reading and learning. In 2016, the Pulitzer Prize for feature writing went to Kathryn Schulz, a writer for *The New Yorker* magazine. Her stellar work told stories about earthquakes and tsunamis, past and future, and the science of measuring them. It is a remarkable work—a marriage of science journalism and literature—that evoked for me the prose of the great Rachel Carson in books such as *The Sea Around Us*.

The measurement of earthquakes on the Richter scale is not easy for me, an English major, to understand. I have learned that because the measurement is "logarithmic," a quake that measures eight is not twice the power of one that measures four. It is many times more powerful than that.

Even more difficult for this civilian to grasp are the tectonic forces below the surface of the earth that cause quakes. I have seen the movie *San Andreas* three times (I like Dwayne Johnson, "The Rock"!), but I can't vouch for its scientific accuracy.

Then I ran into this passage from Schulz:

Take your hands and hold them palms down, middle fingertips touching. Your right hand represents the North American tectonic plate, which bears on its back, among other things, our entire continent, from One World Trade Center to the Space Needle, in Seattle. Your left hand represents an oceanic plate called Juan de Fuca, ninety thousand square miles in size. The place where they meet is the Cascadia subduction zone. [Schulz describes its location in the Northwest earlier in the piece.] Now slide your left hand under your right one. That is what the Juan de Fuca plate is doing: slipping steadily beneath North America. When you try it, your right hand will slide up your left arm, as if you were pushing up your sleeve. That is what North America is not doing. It is stuck, wedged tight against the surface of the other plate.

Without moving your hands, curl your right knuckles up, so that they point toward the ceiling. Under pressure from Juan de Fuca, the stuck edge of North America is bulging upward and compressing eastward, at the rate of, respectively, three to four millimetres and thirty to forty millimetres a year. It can do so for quite some time, because, as continent stuff goes, it is young, made of rock that is still relatively elastic. (Rocks, like us, get stiffer as they age.) But it cannot do so indefinitely. There is a backstop—the craton, that ancient unbudgeable mass at the center of the continent—and, sooner or later, North America will rebound like a spring. If, on that occasion,

> only the southern part of the Cascadia subduction zone gives way—your first two fingers, say—the magnitude of the resulting quake will be somewhere between 8.0 and 8.6. *That's* the big one. If the entire zone gives way at once, an event that seismologists call a full-margin rupture, the magnitude will be somewhere between 8.7 and 9.2. That's the very big one.

I can't express the depth of my appreciation for this passage. But I will try.

Let's return to a practical writer's definition of an analogy. Although it is a comparison, like a metaphor or simile, it is one with an educational or informational intent rather than a literary one. It takes something that is strange to you (the length of a demilitarized zone or the size of the budget deficit) and compares it to something with which you are familiar.

But Schulz takes it one giant step forward. You are invited, in a sense, to act out the analogy, as I did after I read it. Using my palms, fingertips, and knuckles, my science learning became kinetic. This is brainy, crafty, engaging prose. Not all public writers will aspire to that level of creativity. But it still can remind us of the power of the analogy, and invite us to look beyond the football field.

Fiction writers are said to engage in a creative act called "defamiliarization"; that is, they take something familiar—the shape of Gulliver's hat—and make it strange, describing it in a way we have never seen before. More often, public writers are in the business of making the strange feel familiar.

HIGHLIGHTS

- A great tool is the analogy, cousin to the metaphor, which helps readers learn something new by comparing it to something they already understand.
- The most familiar categories of analogy are size, distance, amount, and shape.
- When faced with complex descriptions, the writer should ask "What is this like?" or "What can I compare this to?"
- Keep your reading eyes open for an apt analogy. Keep a file with your favorites. Read them closely to discover what the writer is doing.

23

Tap into the power of the question.

Time after time, when I am looking for examples of civic clarity I turn to the media of sound, from shows produced by public radio to podcasts created by a wide variety of public writers and storytellers. My favorite is National Public Radio's television critic Eric Deggans, whose stories and reports on entertainment, American culture, and race always open new doors of understanding.

Listening to public radio shows such as *Weekend Edition* or *Marketplace* mostly occurs in my car, a 2011 red Toyota Camry with a radio with a faulty volume control. The stories and reports are often so compelling that I experience what NPR refers to as "driveway moments." I may be listening to a segment that has captured my interest as I make my short commute from work. I roll up the driveway, but I don't get out of my car yet. I keep the car on until I hear the end of the story. All public writers should study forms of radio news to get the feel of what clarity and interest *sound* like. Often the most energy derives from the well-asked question.

Versatility of the question mark

The year was 1967, and I was playing the organ in a college rock band called "Tuesday's Children." We were popular in Rhode Island and the surrounding states, playing mixers, sock hops, and frat parties. We made a little spending cash and had lots of fun. We played a gig, a dance concert, at Bryant College (now Bryant University). We played the dance, and a hot band on tour with a hit record played the concert. The hit song was "96 Tears," now a garage-band classic. The band was Question Mark and the Mysterians. If the folks at PolitiFact were to check that out, they would discover a mistake. The band preferred not to spell out its lead singer's rock-and-roll name. They preferred the actual mark of punctuation: "? and the Mysterians."

The inventor of the question mark is said to be an Anglo-Saxon scholar named Alcuin of York, a guy I remember bumping into in graduate school. But who invented the question? My guess is a woman feeling in the interrogative mood, sick and tired of the declarative and imperative moods of the menfolk she encountered. My playful speculation is meant to remind all writers that when it comes to verbs, moods matter. The word *mood* describes a quality of verbs, not to be confused with tense or voice. The mood of a verb describes the environment of meaning in which a verb exists.

In English, the basic moods include the "declarative," sometimes called the mood of reality, the most common way of telling it like it is: "This vaccine will help save your life."

The "imperative" mood is a favorite of parents: "Clean your room"; or of urgent helpers: "Get vaccinated today at the free clinic"; and, too often, of bullies, tyrants, and loud-mouths in general.

The "subjunctive" is the subtlest of moods. It tends to express ambiguity, the hypothetical, or circumstances that are contrary to fact: "If I were you, I'd get vaccinated." To which someone might respond in the declarative: "But you are not me!" The subjunctive pops up in unusual and, at times, archaic phrases, such as "Be that as it may."

What about the interrogative mood?

See what I just did? (I did it again!)

For the purposes of public writing, the question may turn out to be the most versatile and, at its best, the most engaging form of communication. From the question that sparks the advice column to the one that clinches a cross-examination, the question is a communication tool that rules.

Among my favorite uses:

The narrative question: Stories benefit from the energy created by questions, especially those that can be answered only by reading the story: Who done it? Guilty or not guilty? Who wins the race? Who gets the prize? Who is worthy of true love? Who solves the problem? How many obstacles can Harry Potter overcome?

The interview question: In their research, public writers will want to connect with many stakeholders who are affected by a policy or issue. Who has the most at stake? Some stakeholders are official experts: marine biologists, epidemiologists, economists (all those "ist" people). But if you are just asking questions of experts and writing down what they say, you are missing half the game. Every person is an unofficial expert of their own experience. I have overstated it. But there are beneficiaries and victims, winners and losers, even in catastrophes. The best type of interview question, in most cases, is the open-ended question.

The open-ended question: The philosopher Plato made famous the interrogatory teaching style of his famous mentor. We call it the Socratic method, made manifest with the Socratic question. Socrates taught his students by leading them to a predetermined destination, some wisdom about the world or the human condition. The teacher in this case already knows the answer. Questions lead students on a journey toward understanding.

Such questions are not of much use to public writers, except, perhaps, in hard-core investigations to see if a source is telling the truth. With open-ended questions, the source has knowledge that the reporter wants to gain. The questioner does not know the answer ahead of time. That's what makes open-ended questions such a powerful vehicle for learning, collaborating, and gaining on the truth. "You were stranded on the side of the road for hours in that hurricane. What was that like? What did you learn?"

The anticipatory question: I imagine that tour guides over time learn how to anticipate questions: How tall is that building? How long has it been here? Who was the architect? Where is the restroom? In the digital age, this function of anticipation is put into practice on websites by a link to FAQs: Frequently Asked Questions. Those questions do not come out of nowhere. They are harvested by human interaction and algorithms. Done well, they are crucial to public learning and understanding.

The Q&A remains one of the most powerful tools for explanation and comprehension ever created. It anticipates the needs and interests of the audience. It asks questions they would ask, but also ones they would not think to ask. The visual effect of this genre also facilitates the learning. The questions are often set apart typographically—sometimes in boldface. The answers come in digestible chunks.

I am writing this on July 20, 2021, from what used to be the dining room of my house in St. Petersburg, Florida. This space became a home office upon the onset of the COVID-19 pandemic. In recent weeks there has been a resurgence of the Delta variant of the coronavirus. In addition, we have been hit by a small hurricane, Elsa, with some flood damage in the region. There has also been a return of a natural occurrence called a red tide bloom. That tide kills tons and tons of fish and other sea life and fills the air with noxious pollutants.

I had so many questions. It was my good fortune to encounter the work of Zachary T. Sampson and his colleagues at the *Tampa Bay Times*. Their timely Q&A was titled "Tampa Bay has Red Tide questions. Here are some answers." This is not the space to reprint the entire text, but it is worth reprinting the questions. They will offer a quick sense of the scope and complexity of what is being offered to the public:

> What is Red Tide?
> What is a bloom?
> Why is Red Tide plaguing Tampa Bay now?
> Where did this come from? Did the Piney Point disaster have anything to do with it?
> Why is it killing so much marine life?
> When will the bloom go away?
> How long has Red Tide been a problem?
> What role do humans play in a bloom?
> Does Red Tide affect people, too?
> Is it okay to eat seafood right now?
> Can I walk my dog on a beach with Red Tide?
> Can I swim in Red Tide?
> Where is all the dead stuff going?
> This all stinks. What can I do?

I count fifteen questions, accompanied by answers that range from the scientific and technical to the practical. The answer to the question about the Piney Point disaster reveals the level of care in reporting and research:

> This year, scientists say, the Red Tide is almost certainly finding more fuel because of a singular manmade catastrophe: More than 200 million gallons of polluted water was dumped into the bay between late March and early April off the grounds of the old Piney Point fertilizer plant in Manatee County....

> You may have heard local leaders and researchers repeat over and over again that Piney Point did not cause this Red Tide.
>
> What they mean is: The release is not why *Karenia brevis* turned up in the bay. That doesn't mean the pollution couldn't be exacerbating the bloom.
>
> Think of a brush fire: Something has to give off a spark, like a match, to get it going. The flames then need dry material to keep burning. In this case, nutrients—those already in the bay and the enormous amount added by Piney Point—are the fuel.
>
> As for the ignition? Scientists have theorized that several environmental factors may be at play....

A print version of this kind of Q&A can run to a significant length, especially in magazines. Oral histories generated by questions and answers can fill up volumes of books. But there are times when only three or four questions, followed by short answers, suffice.

In broadcast journalism, after a report is delivered, an anchor may "interview" the reporter, a call-and-response that, even when plotted, feels a little like conversation. Public radio makes best use of the form. I especially appreciate questions in reported programs such as *Marketplace*, when the anchor, usually Kai Ryssdal, is trying to unpack a complicated problem with the economy.

Since I began this essay with an anecdote about rock 'n' roll glory, I will end with one on domestic bliss. I can testify that after fifty years of marriage, my wife, Karen, and I know each other's moves—and moods. What I have learned is a strategy that might be called the "imperative interrogative," her order disguised as a question: "Have you put out the trash?"

HIGHLIGHTS

- Public writers cover issues where there are many unanswered questions. Such issues provide opportunities for you to present what you know in a Q&A format.
- Make sure this looks inviting on the screen or the page.
- Take advantage of creative typography to distinguish questions from answers.
- White space will make the text seem more appealing and approachable.
- When you are trying to gain information in an interview, the open-ended question works best, a question where you do not already know the answer: "Can you describe where you were when you first realized there was a fire?"

24

Make all your writing strategies add up and work together.

Clear writing comes from a workbench equipped with a variety of tools. Among them are strategies for thinking, reporting, interviewing, focusing, drafting, and revising as ways of engaging the audience. So far, each chapter has focused on a single strategy that leads to civic clarity. Now it's time to begin to look for what happens in a text when all the parts work together.

Take, for example, a column written by Cass Sunstein for Bloomberg News. It is not often that I find myself invigorated by a 500-word newspaper column, at a level of engagement that leads me to a process I call X-ray reading. I give in to the powerful desire to unveil the text to discover how the writer is working the magic.

My conclusion is that Sunstein has given me a new way of understanding public numbers. It has a name I can easily remember: "anchoring." We know that numbers can be numbing. We are about to see what flashes of insight come to the reader when the writer joins literacy with numeracy.

Sunstein's essay ran in my hometown newspaper, the *Tampa Bay Times*, with the headline "Weighing Trump's 'Anchors.'" Good headline, I think. Anchors aweigh! To reveal the writer's working methods, I will interrupt the text with my annotations.

> Original title: **What Is a 'Very Good Job' on Coronavirus Deaths?**
>
> By Cass Sunstein, Bloomberg News
>
> How many Americans are going to die from the coronavirus? How will we know if the national government or the states have done a commendable job or a terrible one?

There's an archaic taboo against beginning a report or column with a question. Phooey. A question has two benefits: It creates the good illusion of a conversation. And it offers a promise that if you stick with the writer, the question will be answered or clarified.

> Here's a comment from President Donald Trump in late March:
>
> So you're talking about 2.2 million deaths, 2.2 million people from this. And so if we could hold that down, as

> we're saying, to 100,000. It's a horrible number, maybe even less—but to 100,000. So we have between 100- and 200,000, and we altogether have done a very good job.

I don't think it is unfair to refer to that paragraph as a quick case study, an example we are going to learn from. There are six numbers in that short paragraph, which is usually a lot to digest. But even though the president is speaking rather than reading from a text with the clearest syntax, he manages to get his point across. So what's the problem?

> Do you see what Trump did there?

This is my favorite sentence in the column. It comprises seven one-syllable words. It uses the second-person-plural "you" in a question that really feels like we are engaged in some kind of back-and-forth. No, is my answer, I did not see what Trump was doing. But please, if there is some secret business going on here, I need to be in on it.

> It's called "anchoring," and it's one of the most important findings in behavioral science. People who have been involved in real estate, like Trump, are often experts in the use of anchors. Trump specified an anchor (2.2 million deaths), and he used it to support his claim that if 100,000 to 200,000 Americans end up dying, he has "done a very good job."

This feels effective to me for two reasons. First, he introduces us to a new term, a bit of jargon—but also a metaphor—to let us in to the secret club with the secret passwords. Second, the writer doesn't squeeze everything about anchors into this space. He is controlling the pace of information, introducing a new concept. It does not feel like I am being lectured to here, even with the phrase "behavioral science." It feels more like sitting across from a smart friend at a coffee shop who is sketching out something I need to know on a paper napkin.

> Whenever the goal is to affect people's evaluations, it's smart to get a particular number in their heads, whether it involves pricing property or estimating deaths. That number often sticks. It influences their judgments about what's likely or what's fair, and about what counts as a successful outcome or instead a disaster.

Having led us to the edge of the shore, the writer guides us into the water, but only up to our knees. The language in this paragraph is fairly neutral, almost as if the writer is a helpful coach about to teach us how to swim. The two clauses that stand out are "it's smart to get a particular number in their heads" and another short sentence, "That number often sticks." Clever writers often save their best thought for their shortest sentence. Short sentences ring true.

> Here's an example from law. Suppose you are a lawyer, and some defective product (say, an exercise machine) malfunctioned and seriously hurt your client. Suppose that you're suing the manufacturer not only for medical bills, but also for "pain and suffering."

> To capture that harm, it's tough for a jury (or, for that matter, a judge) to come up with a specific monetary figure. But if you can get a large number in their minds—say $900 million in annual sales, or $300 million in annual profits—you can influence judgments in your client's favor. Jurors might even think: "They can earn $300 million a year. Let's give just 1% of that: $3 million!" In a catchphrase, "The more you ask for, the more you get." That's a tribute to the power of anchoring.

I don't have a particular name for this move so I will give you three: a side trip, a turn down a side street, a subplot. It is healthy for the writer to present evidence that sounds more neutral than a standard critique of the president. The move from politics and medicine to the law expands the evidence and demonstrates the broader utility of understanding the anchor. It's dangerous to clutter numbers, but these come in a mini-narrative that is somewhat familiar, even if distorted by television dramas. "That's a tribute to the power of anchoring" is another important short sentence, and the writer places it strategically at the end of the paragraph to intensify the emphasis. Let's skip ahead a few paragraphs:

> Which brings us back to COVID-19. To say the least, it's not simple to know whether a specific number of deaths is a success or a failure.

I find this structure appealing: Begin with COVID-19, transition to the law, return to the disease. This feeling that the parts fit together is called "coherence." Signposts from the writer—"Which brings us back"—help the reader stay on the path. I admire the humility of "it's not simple to know."

> If the anchor is 2.2 million deaths from the coronavirus—if that's what could have happened—then 200,000 might look like a spectacular achievement. After all, two million deaths have been prevented.
>
> If the anchor is 56,000—the approximate number of Americans who die from the flu each year—then that same 200,000 figure looks really bad.
>
> And if the anchor is lower than 56,000—perhaps the number if the U.S. government had responded promptly and aggressively—then 100,000 deaths is a catastrophic failure.

Note the parallel structure of these three paragraphs. Each is organized with an "if...then" pattern. If this were the anchor, then this would be the effect. That structure might not even be noticed by the reader (I did not notice it in my first reading). It still works to lead the audience in a step-by-step process of understanding the numbers. Three is the largest number in writing. When a writer uses three examples, that writer is sending the message "this is all you need to know."

> The lesson is simple. Don't be fooled by anchors.

I don't think the lesson is that simple. But the idea does not offend me. It is a word of encouragement to citizens reading the essay: If you have read this far, I hope that you have learned the moral of the story: "Don't be fooled by anchors." These two consecutive short sentences slow the reader down in a good way.

> To evaluate Trump's performance, and that of the U.S. government, we have to ask what, exactly, was done, and what might have been done differently. And if we do that, it's a pretty good bet that if the United States ends up with over 100,000 deaths, national officials did not do a "very good job."

It makes sense that the writer would take the argument full circle. He begins with the virus, number of deaths, and the president. And he ends that way, with a conclusion appropriate to the evidence. Others may disagree. (As of early November 2022, the United States had logged nearly 1,097,000 deaths from COVID.)

HIGHLIGHTS

Here is my list of tools the writer uses to teach us the potentially exploitive strategy of anchoring. A good teacher takes responsibility for what the student understands. To achieve civic clarity, the writer:

- Uses short sentences for emphasis
- Uses word order for emphasis
- Begins with a question to propel the issue
- Introduces us to a new concept to help us see numbers in a new way

- Translates jargon or technical language
- Uses parallel structures to create an easy pattern for evaluating numbers
- Uses a "case study" to test his ideas
- Chooses three examples as a sign of completeness
- Uses the word *you* to create the feel of interaction with the audience
- Presents evidence of anchoring from more than one field of endeavor
- Establishes an accessible pace of information, created by a variety of shorter sentences

Part II

Telling Stories

In February 2022, while I was in the final stages of writing this book, Russia invaded Ukraine. This unprovoked war upon a small democratic nation by an autocratic superpower shocked and outraged much of the world. In support of his own propaganda efforts, the Russian president shut down forms of media that were not servile to his vicious interests. He was not waging a war, Vladimir Putin lied; he was not attacking civilians, he lied again; he was just conducting a military exercise.

But news from Ukraine spread throughout the world. It was conveyed by courageous war correspondents, some of whom gave their lives to the cause. It was delivered by the spirited and resilient president of Ukraine, Volodymyr Zelenskyy, who made a virtual appearance before the US Congress.

It emerged from citizens of Ukraine, some in the midst of their brave resistance, some during their dramatic escapes from war zones.

The news came in the form of reports, filled with maps, arrows, numbers—the number of troops, the number of tanks, the number of missiles, the number of refugees. But, more powerfully, the news came in the form of stories, the shared experiences of what it was like to be there, under attack, your city destroyed, your world turned upside down. A bomb hits a maternity hospital. A woman, about to give birth, is severely injured. She fears that her unborn child is dead. "Kill me now," she says, shortly before her own passing. Doctors try to save the baby, but they can't.

Telling it like it is requires more than factual reporting. It requires stories, narratives that help us see it, smell it, live it.

I have worked with many public writers in recent years and have discovered that most have the same aspirations. They want to improve in their craft and sharpen their sense of mission and purpose. As writers, they want to learn these four things:

- How to make hard facts easy reading
- How to make important things interesting so that readers will pay attention
- How to find an authentic writing voice that, while distinctive, is in harmony with the enterprise they represent
- How to tell good stories in the public interest

This section is devoted to that last item—storytelling. What makes a story good? That question becomes increasingly important in an age of pandemic, social unrest, economic decline, mass shootings, insurrection, and disinformation, and, most recently, the Russian invasion of Ukraine. What follows is an attempt to answer that question, distilled from many conversations with journalists and public writers.

25

Embrace storytelling as a virtue.

I've heard a theory that suggests that human beings need stories to remember, that we may not be able to remember anything as little kids until we have been exposed to stories; then we can craft stories out of our own experience. Part of my own sense of memory is that I reach into a dusty file in my brain for the name of an old song or the author of a book. But I also envision my past as a kind of narrative, a movie in which I am the main character. God or Darwin or both gave us a brain of a certain size. That brain gave us language. Language led to stories, a form of human expression that can be delivered, amazingly, as either fiction or nonfiction. In the public sense, argues scholar Brian Boyd, stories contribute to our survival, pointing us to the dangers we must avoid and the helpers who can get us out of trouble.

So what makes a good story "good," and a bad story "bad"? This is a crucial question. In spite of the power and value of stories in our culture, I believe that narrative itself is morally neutral. A story is a "verbal contraption" (to borrow an idea and phrase from the poet W. H. Auden) with a person inside. If that person is guided by noble purpose, there's a greater chance the story will be good. But genocidal tyrants use some of the same strategies of craft that responsible writers use for the public good. We will argue, of course, over what constitutes a noble purpose. My advice to writers is to have a stated mission for every text you write.

HIGHLIGHTS

- You can write a big mission statement, as for this book: "I want more and more scribes to see themselves as public writers and to embrace the strategies that best serve the common good."
- You can also write a smaller mission statement, for an essay or a chapter: "I want the reader of this chapter to understand the difference between a report and a story, and to understand the effect of each on a reader."
- If *mission* is too weighty a word for you, try *goal*, instead. Ask yourself "What is my goal in writing this?" "Why am I writing this?" "What good do I hope will come from this?"

26

Learn the crucial difference between reports and stories.

The distinction between reports and stories is clear—at least in my head. We call too many things we produce "stories." Many of them are reports: information delivered so that others can act on it. The purpose of a story is not to convey information but to capture experience. A report tells me how many gallons of oil are polluting the Gulf. A story transports me to a boat where old fishermen and women are working to save the shoreline. Whatever media platform you work from, you are not creating a story unless you are helping the reader or viewer or listener feel what it is like to be there. That effect can only be produced from tested strategies: details that define character; action delivered in a sequence of scenes; dialogue, rather than simple quotes or sound bites; a purposeful variety of points of view.

Let's drill down on the crucial distinction between reports and stories:

- The report delivers information in the public interest; the story is a form of virtual experience.
- The report tells who was involved; the story turns the who into a character.
- The report tells you what happened in a summary; the story tells you what happened in a sequence of scenes.
- The report tells you where something happened; the story turns the where into a setting.
- The report lets you know when something happened; the story turns a timeline into action.
- The report, with difficulty, informs you why something occurred; the story explores not a single cause but several possible causes and effects.

HIGHLIGHTS

- As you prepare to write a text, ask yourself if your primary purpose is to create a report or a story.
- If you are not confident about writing full stories, begin by writing anecdotes, short story elements often used at the beginning of an article to hook readers.
- An effective structure for combining reports and

stories is called the "broken line." It usually begins with an anecdote, followed by information or explanation, returning to a bit of narrative.

- Use story elements as gold coins, rewards for the reader who is moving through some challenging information.

27

Remember, "the bigger, the smaller."

In the best public writing, short and long forms support each other. Stories have titles or headlines. Photos have captions. PowerPoint presentations combine the short form of the slide into what can become a long sequence of slides.

In both stories and reports, the anecdote, as we've mentioned, is a favored tool. Readers and writers tend to embrace the anecdote—or little story—as a way to encapsulate that part of the world they are covering. The little story, if well chosen, represents the whole. But we all know that anecdotes can be chosen for their dramatic power rather than their representational value.

To repeat, reports deliver information to readers; stories create experiences. You can convey experience in an anecdote even if it takes only a paragraph, maybe even in just a couple of sentences. "They banged on a garbage can in the dugout so the hitter knew he was getting a curveball." You can experience that, even though I delivered it in a few words. Or "I walked around the mile track and noticed seven lost or discarded medical masks. In thirty years of walking that track, I had never seen one before."

Early in the pandemic, I asked my wife how many rolls of toilet paper we had in the house. She guessed twenty. I searched and found fifty-two, none of them purchased in a panic. "It's just BOGO," she said (Buy One, Get One Free). That's a tiny story from my own experience during a global hoarding of toilet paper.

The late Jim Dwyer, who wrote for the *New York Times*, taught me a lesson he learned from a city editor: "The bigger, the smaller." It may be hard to get a handle on a subject as complex as "the American bureaucracy," or "the effects of inflation on the American people," or "the economic impact of high technology on previously underserved rural areas." One key to writing and reporting such a story is to find a specific, concrete example that represents the larger reality.

"I know there's a problem with vandalism in the county schools," says the editor to the reporter. "But isn't there one school we can focus on to tell the story?" Or "It looks like more top students are starting their college careers at junior colleges. Let's make sure we identify a student and a family—or three students and three families—to build a story around."

The word *microcosm*, meaning "little world," derives from the Greek. The idea is that a little world represents a bigger world, a "macrocosm" if you will. Fiction writers offer us countless examples of the microcosm, from literature to popular culture, going back to the Middle Ages. Chaucer sent thirty pilgrims, a cross-section of English society, into a tavern together, then on horseback to Canterbury. The great American novelist Lauren Groff wrote a novel set in upstate New York in the 1970s about a group of characters living in a commune: *Arcadia*. Then she wrote *Matrix* about a charismatic proto-feminist nun who heads an abbey in twelfth-century England. Create a little world. Invite readers in.

After the attacks of 9/11, Dwyer wrote a series of stories based on articles related to the destruction of the Twin Towers. A window washer's squeegee, a family photo that fluttered from a high office into the rubble, a Styrofoam cup of water given by one stranger to another. Find an object with a story hiding inside it.

In that spirit, Jennifer Senior won a 2022 Pulitzer Prize for feature writing for her story in *The Atlantic* about the enduring grief of a family that lost a son on 9/11. Twenty years later that loss was encapsulated in a diary that had been left behind, among a pile of writings—a diary that Bobby McIlvaine's father gave to his son's fiancé. Senior writes:

> One object in that pile glowed with more meaning than all the others: Bobby's very last diary. Jen took one look and quickly realized that her name was all over it. Could she keep it?

The mystery of what messages were contained in those few pages became the powerful engine for a story about loss, memory, regret, and the hope for reconciliation. The bigger, the smaller. And the smaller the bigger.

HIGHLIGHTS

- Don't be intimidated by a big topic. Look for a small entry point.
- That entry point can be a person who exemplifies a group or a place that captures what is happening in other places.
- The entry point can also be an object — an heirloom, a photo, a garment — with a story hiding inside it.
- Remember the words of the poet T. S. Eliot, who said that the writer is always searching for the "objective correlative" — an object or moment that correlates to the emotion you are trying to express.
- A long report can be spiced with anecdotes.
- An anecdote can grow into a long story.

28

Descend into the underworld.

There is an ancient hero story that has many faces. It is sometimes called the Descent into the Underworld. In Greek mythology, for example, Orpheus enters the underworld in order to bring his love Eurydice back to the world of the living. These myths and archetypes are so deep and so enduring—crossing centuries and cultures—that it should not surprise us to find them appearing not just in the narratives of popular culture but also in nonfiction, journalism, and other expressions of public writing and storytelling.

Perhaps the most famous expression of this narrative appears in Dante's *Divine Comedy* (1320), which begins with a descent into the Inferno, or hell. In the story the poet finds himself in a bad place, a dark wood, where he experiences a crisis of the soul. He meets a guide—who happens to be

Virgil—Italy's greatest poet and author of the epic poem the *Aeneid.* "Lay aside all hope, ye who enter here," is the sign over the mouth of hell. But with Virgil's help, Dante descends down, down into the nine circles of hell, deeper and deeper as the sinners he meets become more notorious, their sins more vicious, their punishments more painful.

A three-faced Satan sits at the frigid center of hell with the three greatest sinners in his mouths: Judas, who betrayed Jesus; and Cassius and Brutus, who conspired to assassinate Julius Caesar. Dante will survive this terrible place and make his ascent into Purgatory and finally into Paradise.

In nonfiction the underworld can be literal—workers trapped in a mine disaster, homeless people sleeping in the subway tunnels under New York City, a youth soccer team stuck in a flooded cave in Thailand. But the underworld can also be metaphorical. Let's take, for example, the intensive care units of hospitals filled with patients suffering, even near death, unable to breathe. Imagine the nightmare it would be to enter that world, either as a patient or a caregiver.

From television reports on the effects of COVID, I have an idea of the crowded environment and grim prospects of the ill, most of whom, it turns out, were unvaccinated. Frustrating are commentaries from patients: "If I had only known I would wind up in this hell, I would have made different choices."

What does hell look like and feel like? Dante gives us his view of the cosmos and the afterlife. For this moment, and this chapter, our Dante—and maybe also our guiding Virgil—is Karen Gallardo, a respiratory therapist at a hospital in Ventura, California. She also happens to be a public writer of considerable skill. What she offered through the *Los Angeles Times* was her contemporary version of the nine circles of hell. She calls them the seven stages of severe COVID.

I can imagine a kind of civic purpose growing out of the Descent archetype. It might be stated this way: "Here is what is waiting for you as a consequence of irresponsible actions." In high school, we were shown *Death on the Highway* films with grotesque images of corpses of those killed in auto accidents as a result of careless or drunken driving. The military would show soldiers explicit films of what sexually transmitted diseases did to the body. And, of course, there was *Reefer Madness*, a now-funny take on the dangers of the wacky weed, so, as always, these tropes can be applied inauthentically.

Here is Karen Gallardo:

> I'm a respiratory therapist. With the fourth wave of the pandemic in full swing, fueled by the highly contagious Delta variant, the trajectory of the patients I see, from admission to critical care, is all too familiar. When they're vaccinated, their COVID-19 infections most likely end after Stage 1. If only that were the case for everyone.
>
> Get vaccinated. If you choose not to, here's what to expect if you are hospitalized for a serious case of COVID-19.

What you should expect is a descent into hell.

Like an illustrated map of Dante's *Inferno*, the column appears in seven numbered sections for each stage of descent.

Each section is two or three short paragraphs, but I will summarize them by quoting single sentences.

> Stage 1. You've had debilitating symptoms for a few days, but now it is so hard to breathe that you... need help, a supplemental flow of 1 to 4 liters of oxygen per minute....
>
> Stage 2. It becomes harder and harder for you to breathe. "Like drowning," many patients describe the feeling....
>
> Stage 3. You're exhausted from hyperventilating to satisfy your body's demand for air....
>
> Stage 4. Your breathing becomes even more labored. We can tell you're severely fatigued. An arterial blood draw confirms that the oxygen content in your blood is critically low. We prepare to intubate you. If you're able to and if there's time, we will suggest that you call your loved ones. This might be the last time they'll hear your voice....
>
> Stage 5. Some patients survive Stage 4....
>
> Stage 6. The pressure required to open your lungs is so high that air can leak into your chest cavity, so we insert tubes to clear it out....
>
> Stage 7. After several meetings with the palliative care team, your family decides to withdraw care.

If all this sounds horrific, know that I am leaving out the more gruesome details of medical care—if that level of care is even available under conditions of crowding. Here's what happens at the very end: "As we work in your room, we hear crying and loving goodbyes. We cry, too, and we hold your hand until your last natural breath." Gallardo offers this valediction to readers: "I've been at this for 17 months now. It doesn't get easier. My pandemic stories rarely end well."

Maybe it's unfair or inaccurate to refer to Karen Gallardo as a hero in the mythological sense, although she may be well considered one in the community sense. In the great myths, the hero escapes the underworld and raises the loved one. It appears for the present that she is stuck in hell, attending to the nearly dead for as long as she can.

In doing so, she renders a form of public writing that deserves a name. This is inelegant, but perhaps it is a "narrative of unforeseen consequences." More than a cautionary tale, her story suggests a fatal punishment for those who fail to seek lifesaving measures, including vaccines, that could lead us out of the Dark Wood of COVID and its excruciating effects.

HIGHLIGHTS

- It is no surprise that during times of great social trauma — wars, pandemics, environmental disasters, political protests, terrorism, and mass shootings — public writers will find themselves, in the words of Joseph Conrad, immersed "in the destructive element."
- Protect yourself, physically and emotionally, when writing about dangerous times.
- As Dante found Virgil, find a guide, a person who can

lead you through a difficult world, introduce you to key players, and coach you on the process you will be describing.

- Even when it is too perilous to enter a danger zone, you can look for a victim or first responder or caregiver who can share what it was like to be there.
- There are stages of danger or trauma or escape that will allow you to shape a narrative.
- The hell you describe does not have to be literal and vast. It can be metaphorical and personal.

29

Write in service of public ritual.

In spite of social distancing, the news of the pandemic years has often been defined by crowds. Emergency rooms stuffed to the point of triage. Humans cramming testing or vaccination sites. Small armies of protesters marching for social justice. Insurrectionists swarming the Capitol. The National Guard protecting the inauguration. A million refugees fleeing Ukraine.

Less visible by definition, but just as important, is not the emptiness of news, but the news of emptiness.

No expression of journalism will mark that tension between crowdedness and emptiness better than the Sunday, February 21, 2021, front page of the *New York Times*, especially the dramatic graphic and the accompanying story by Julie Bosman. The data graphic is an exercise in informational and emotional pointillism. In nineteenth-century art, French painters would use tiny points of paint to create an impression of a scene or landscape. On the front page of the paper that day, each point represented a death from COVID-19, one of almost 500,000.

The visual effect is that of a monolith, an eerie, morbid two-dimensional column of print. Following the time markers, the earlier months look grayer with some white space visible. As the pandemic roars toward the present, the points become more crowded and the image becomes almost black—a shadow of death.

In typography, a block of impenetrable gray type is called a tombstone. This image is a tombstone for the lost, a twin tower before its collapse.

It is the language of loss that marks the diction (the total effect of words chosen) in the accompanying story by Julie Bosman, assisted in reporting by four colleagues. In many ways, Bosman's story is as remarkable and unusual as the graphic, news that transcends daily reportage. She begins with a wise decision: to liberate the startling truths of the pandemic from the chains of decorative language, creating the effect that the facts speak for themselves:

> CHICAGO—A nation numbed by misery and loss is confronting a number that still has the power to shock: 500,000.
>
> Roughly one year since the first known death by the coronavirus in the United States, an unfathomable toll is nearing—the loss of half a million people.
>
> No other country has counted so many deaths in the

> pandemic. More Americans have perished from Covid-19 than on the battlefields of World War I, World War II and the Vietnam War combined.
>
> The milestone comes at a hopeful moment: New virus cases are down sharply, deaths are slowing and vaccines are steadily being administered.
>
> But there is concern about emerging variants of the virus, and it may be months before the pandemic is contained.

Numbers are often underappreciated as elements of news and narrative, but, as the number *six million* signifies the Holocaust, *500,000* earns a place at the end of the first sentence, a position where no reader can ignore it. At the end of the next paragraph, the number is repeated but with humanity attached: "the loss of half a million people."

The writer may not have intended it, but her repetition of the word *loss*, which also appears in the headline, is a real-life answer to questions we've asked for decades in writing workshops: "What is your story really about? Can you say it in one word?"

If you read Bosman's story, you will notice how often the language of loss appears with creative and purposeful repetition and variation, a monolith of language. It gains momentum with her next two paragraphs:

> Each death has left untold numbers of mourners, a ripple effect of loss that has swept over towns and cities. Each death has left an empty space in communities across

> America: a bar stool where a regular used to sit, one side of a bed unslept in, a home kitchen without its cook.
>
> The living find themselves amid vacant places once occupied by their spouses, parents, neighbors and friends—the nearly 500,000 coronavirus dead.

Listen to the language: *loss*, *empty space*, *used to sit*, *unslept in*, *without*, *vacant places*.... It continues on and on deep into the story.

With the help of her colleagues, the writer flies virtually across the nation and descends to find the deeply human absence experienced by survivors of the lost, to give names to a few of the dead. By "landing" in cities across the landscape, she creates a sense of national and universal loss, one of the few times in the current moment when, whatever our divisions, we can feel the suffering of others.

Toward the end of the story, Bosman quotes a funeral director who finds himself using the same language to describe what he has experienced through the pandemic:

> "People are feeling a psychological and spiritual void," said Paddy Lynch, a funeral director in Michigan who has worked with families who have lost relatives to the coronavirus.
>
> Part of that void, he said, comes from the missing rituals, the lack of a communal catharsis after a death.

Listen to the language, like a tolling bell: *void*, *lost*, *missing*, *lack*, *death*.

It is clear that the *Times* was not merely delivering information to readers. There was something going on beyond that, an example of a theory of news articulated by one of journalism's great scholars, the late James Carey. He talked about the ritual function of news, in which journalism brings the community together—in the case of a Super Bowl victory, to celebrate, and, in the case of a pandemic, to mourn. I know this line of thinking will be ridiculed, but I truly believe that Bosman and her colleagues, and the data illustrators who created the graphic, are playing a role more commonly assigned to priests and rabbis, to eulogists and elegists, to homilists and hagiographers. They offer realization but also consolation, a vision of shared humanity marked by tragedy, hope, and, yes, loss.

As humans, we crave ritual and ceremony. We need them to comfort us, reward us, express our shared values, and build a community upon which we can depend. Of all the losses marked by the pandemic, among the greatest are the losses of ceremony. Social distancing meant that proms, birthdays, anniversaries, graduations, concerts, weddings, funerals, public celebrations, athletic events—all had to wait.

When we think of the experience of public writing, it rarely includes the idea of ritual. More of habit, perhaps. To use Carey's distinction, we are more likely to think of the transmission of information. Writers go out and find things out and check things out and transmit the most important and interesting stuff to our eyes and ears. In the interests of self-government, that act seems essential. But that act of transmission is not likely—this is my opinion—to help people love their community. That feeling of love requires something more. It requires ritual. Only public writers can write the script for the ceremony.

HIGHLIGHTS

• Two things can happen when you are writing a report or story: you can transmit information in the public interest; you can also create an effect that the reader is participating in a shared ritual.

• The language of ritual tends to sound more rhetorical, even liturgical at times. Think repetition of key words, such as *loss* above. Think parallel construction. Think a slower, more dramatic pace, created by shorter sentences. Think emphatic word order, with key words or phrases appearing at the end.

• *The Godfather* movie begins with a wedding and ends with a christening, conducted as a series of mob hits are under way. Storytelling in all forms contains scenes in which common rituals bring characters together—for better or worse. The most common are weddings, funerals, graduation ceremonies, birthday parties, holiday gatherings, athletic competitions, concerts, and bar mitzvahs. Look for these and others to include in your research and writing.

• Writing for public rituals should influence your word selection—what we call "diction." Depending on whether you are striving for celebration or mourning, work to choose words that are appropriate for the occasion.

• Have you ever watched a movie that shows a wedding

or a funeral and found yourself crying? We know the event is not real and the characters are actors, yet we can feel an emotional catharsis. That trick is as old as the ancient Greek dramas, and should help you remember that power you have as a writer and storyteller.

30

Frame your story as a mystery to solve.

With so much misinformation hitting us, it is a tribute to the work of public writers—across the globe—that so much information is reliable. Disinformation and propaganda aside, we will always find mistakes in reports: false assumptions, lack of context, numbers that don't quite add up. In my experience, these are mostly failures of time, resources, and process and almost never the result of an intent to distort or misinform. The question for me, then, is not what to believe. I trust my various "reliable sources." It's what to read. So much news and information, so little time.

When public writers capture my attention, I always ask the question "How did they do it?"

A case in point arrived the morning of March 8, 2021, in

a digital newsletter from the *New York Times*. Written by the lionhearted David Leonhardt, it began with this greeting above the headline:

> **Good morning. Why has Covid's toll been surprisingly low across much of Africa and Asia?**

I can't say how much I appreciate the "Good morning." Maybe it's the text version of a news anchor greeting you on your favorite morning show. It turns a potentially presentational tone into a more conversational one. That is, it imagines the presence of a real audience. That effect of conversation is magnified by what comes next—a question. "Why has Covid's toll been surprisingly low across much of Africa and Asia?"

I remember advice from a news curmudgeon that you should never raise a question at the beginning of a story that you are unprepared to answer for the reader. So, yes, I find that question fascinating. And, yes, I want to know the answer. Maybe I am wearing blinders. Maybe my narrow Western perspective would just assume that those other countries, way over there, would have a worse go of it when it came to all forms of health care.

The *Times* lifts the heavy cargo of data from the text and places it in a simple chart. It shows that deaths per million are highest in Great Britain, America, and Italy and quite low in Pakistan, Vietnam, and Nigeria. How to explain those differences?

That question is captured in a phrase by Siddhartha Mukherjee: "An epidemiological whodunnit."

Such an unusual phrase deserves some attention. It gains its energy from the juxtaposition of two long words that you don't often see together. That kind of language friction is an old writer's trick that you will find in countless titles, such as *The Great Gatsby* and my own *The Glamour of Grammar.*

To understand that phrase—to "get it," if you will—requires a fairly high degree of previous knowledge on the part of the reader. Remember that a reader's previous knowledge is one of the most significant determiners of comprehensibility. If I am a fan of the English football club Arsenal—and understand the offside rule—I am more likely to find, read, and grasp an article on a controversial call in an important match.

No writer or editor can know in advance the level of a particular reader's previous knowledge. But it is something that deserves attention, even if it leads to an educated guess. How much do I think my reader knows and understands about this topic? Can I assume after a year of COVID that readers know what *COVID* means? What *pandemic* means? Who Dr. Fauci is? What *epidemiology* means? It took me most of a year to realize that *epidemiology* has the word *epidemic* hiding inside it. So epidemiologists are scientists who specialize in epidemics—outbreaks of contagious diseases that spread widely and quickly. By now many people know that a pandemic is not confined to a region but is widespread.

People who understand the word *epidemiological* are brainy enough to understand the word *whodunnit*, even though it's a weird mashup of the ungrammatical question "Who done it?" My dictionary spells it with one *n*—"whodunit"—and defines it as an informal term for a story dealing with "crime and its solution."

Writer Tom French calls a question like "Who done it?" an "engine" for a story. The question "What is the meaning of 'Rosebud'?" generates the action in the movie *Citizen Kane.* Who done it? Guilty or not guilty? Who will win the prize? Or, if you are into dragons and such, Who will sit on the Iron Throne? But also: When will I be able to get a vaccine? Is one vaccine better than another? And, yes, why are countries in Africa and Asia so far having a better time of it when it comes to COVID deaths, and is there anything we can learn from their circumstances?

There are responsible and irresponsible ways to use the strategy of the "mystery" to generate interest in a story. I can't count the times I've fallen victim to headlines or teasers—sometimes referred to as "clickbait." Any headline that begins "You'll never guess what happened when…" or "Why they don't want you to see…" or "You'll never feel the same way again after…" Add a bizarre or provocative image, and there goes my cursor, headed for the link.

As a writer, I must plead guilty to the venial sin I am describing. When you traffic in grammar and punctuation, as I often do, it helps to sprinkle a little pixie dust on the cow pie. How about a headline such as "What they don't want you to know about the semicolon"? Or "How a secret cabal at the AP is standing between you and the Oxford comma"? It helps to be able to attract a crowd, even a little one. Call it clickbait for nerds.

We all want to learn secrets, especially juicy ones, like

out of Buckingham Palace. But there are people in power—some with ill intent—who want to keep secrets from us. That makes the revelation of secrets in the public interest central to the mission of reporters, investigators, and public writers.

I have argued that when it comes to answering the questions readers want answered, public writers are much better at the *Who*, *What*, *Where*, and *When* than they are the *Why*. When it comes to motive, human beings are often opaque, and writers often fall victim to the logical fallacy of the single motive or single cause.

What works so well in the *New York Times* summary is a logical list of answers to the question *Why?* when it comes to differences in the rate of fatalities between West and East. That list, marked by subheads, seemed so clear, in fact, that I am going to give the reasons here as I remember them—but not in order. It's a great test of comprehensibility.

1. Western countries have older populations, more nursing homes, a lower birth rate, with more people vulnerable to COVID.
2. The climate in many Asian and African countries is warmer, so people are more likely to spend more of their time outdoors, in well-ventilated spaces, less vulnerable to crowded workplaces where infections can more easily spread.
3. Western countries, where freedom of movement is more part of the culture, are less likely to adopt and enforce restrictive policies that help slow the spread

of the disease. In countries like Ghana, there is less freedom — and less death.

4. "Immunity may not be uniform," which means that populations in some countries — with more frequent exposure to microbes — may have developed stronger immunities over time.

OK, that's what I remember. A good test of whether a writer has achieved civic clarity in a report is whether readers can remember key points.

Without ramming home some "mystery solved" conclusion, Leonhardt carries the trope to a reasonable if undramatic conclusion:

> The full answer to this mystery surely involves multiple explanations. Whatever they are, it's one of the few ways in which Covid has not been as bad as many had feared. Hundreds of thousands of people across Africa and Asia have still died of this terrible disease. But many others are alive today for reasons that are both unclear and marvelous.

HIGHLIGHTS

- Anyone can make interesting things seem important. (Watch cable news much?) Instead, work on making the important interesting.
- Raise questions for readers that the story will answer. If you are good at it, you can frame these questions as secrets to be exposed or mysteries to be solved.

- You can do this without hype. No clickbaiting allowed. (OK, once a year.)
- The greatest predictor of engagement with and comprehensibility of a text is the reader's level of previous knowledge. You can't know it. But you can attend to it and make educated guesses.

31

Avoid the fallacy of the single cause.

We were driving through Tampa one Sunday afternoon in May of 2021 feeling some freedom of movement when millions of Americans had been vaccinated against the coronavirus. Restaurants and other small businesses were beginning to reopen. We noticed "Now Hiring" signs everywhere, a bounce back from the Now Firing realities of the pandemic.

But there was a wrinkle to common expectations. Businesses, especially small businesses, were finding it hard to find workers. Why weren't they lining up to fill now-available jobs? The answer to that question, the hardest question in public writing—*Why?*—turned out to have competing answers, predictably one from the Right and one from the Left.

The challenge from the Right was that too-generous payments from unemployment insurance were creating a welfare system in which workers chose to get paid for not working rather than put their shoulders to the wheel. One response from the Left was that the pay being offered to workers was too low, at times barely scraping the minimum wage. Stingy employers were the problem.

One of the only lessons I remember from a college logic class was this: avoid the fallacy of the single cause. Maybe in mystery fiction it is possible for a writer to imagine a single, big cause for a crime. But to tell it like it is often requires the answer "We are not sure."

Good public writers have identified multiple causes for the employment issue: 1) the extended payment of unemployment checks, 2) low wages offered by employers, 3) the need for child care when children were attending virtual classes from home, 4) fear of contracting COVID-19 at a time when there was confusion about who was vaccinated and whether a company was enforcing mitigation efforts such as wearing masks and social distancing, and 5) unemployed workers acquiring new skills for better jobs. Somewhere in that constellation of reasons we never reach certainty of motive, but we gain on it.

In no cycle of news stories and public events is uncertainty more prevalent than in mass shootings, a plague of violent deaths that, more and more, define a dark side of American culture. There have been seemingly countless mass shootings during the years I have been writing this book. They have occurred on city streets, in nightclubs, in grocery stores, in theaters and at concert venues, in houses of worship, even in elementary schools, where we have had to collectively endure the slaughter of little children.

A man, a gambler, rents a room in a tourist hotel in Las Vegas. It overlooks the site of a music festival. He lugs guns and ammunition to his room. He begins to fire into the crowd, killing dozens of people and injuring more, as the crowd scurries for cover. It is one of the largest mass shootings in modern American history. But why, why, why?

Now, years later, there is no clear motive for the shooting. The killer had been a gambler. His father had been a notorious bank robber. He had access to lots of weapons. None of those elements lead inevitably to those horrible crimes. And we can't interrogate his motive because, as often happens, the killer took his own life before he could be apprehended.

Here is a list of reasons commonly offered for acts of mass murder:

1. He (almost always a he) suffered from mental illness.
2. He had access to guns, bombs, other weapons.
3. He had a grudge against: the business, the church, the school.
4. He was a disgruntled employee.
5. He was the victim of abuse or bullying.
6. He had a political or other ideological motive.
7. He hated Black people, Asian people, gay people, Jews, women, cops, Muslims, you name them.
8. His wife, partner, girlfriend broke up with him.
9. He craved notoriety.

Scholar Stephen Greenblatt, who has won a Pulitzer Prize for general nonfiction and who is an effective and influential public scholar, notes that one of the hallmarks of

Shakespeare's genius was the "opacity of motive." The Bard gave blurry answers to the question *Why?* Why is Hamlet so slow in finding his way to avenge his father? Why did Iago hate Othello so much that he was moved to plot a murder and his downfall? Greenblatt points out that in Shakespeare's source material, there is often a clear answer to the question. Shakespeare decided it makes a better story if the motive is not Hollywood clear.

No algorithm of reporting is more enduring and productive than the Five *Ws*: *Who*, *What*, *Where*, *When*, and *Why*. None of those is harder to answer than the *Why*. After following the news of the mass killing in Las Vegas, I made a mental list of what I thought I knew, and what I so much wanted to learn.

The Who: We know the identity of the killer and many details of his life. We know about the dead and injured, the first responders, musicians on the stage, the investigators, the spontaneous helpers and heroes. We know of his girlfriend in the Philippines. Her sisters and his brothers. The president of the United States. The head of the NRA. With so many Whos available, the job of the public writer is to choose the ones most interesting, most important, or most relevant to a particular angle of the story.

The What: We know about the shooter's actions and their effects. We know about the fear and chaos they caused. How the shootings moved people to escape or to rescue others. We know what happened when a security guard—followed by a SWAT team—made their way to the thirty-second floor of the hotel, from which the killer looked down on a concert crowd and picked out his targets.

The Where: We know Las Vegas. The Strip. Mandalay Bay. The country music concert venue. The parking lot where they found his car. The random places where people took cover. The insides of ambulances. The packed hospitals engaged in triage of the victims.

The When: We know when the shooter checked into the hotel. When he started shooting. How long he was firing into the crowd. When they figured out what room he was in. When he shot himself. By now we have several timelines that attempt to measure the chronologies of his preparations and actions, as well as responses to them.

The Why: We do not know the answer, and, what is difficult to accept, we may never know in a way that all stakeholders and the public feel they need to know. No wonder the great scholar of democracy and culture James Carey once referred to the Why as the dark, unexplored territory of American journalism:

> Why answers to the question of explanation. It accounts for events, actions, and actors. It is a search for the deeper factors that lie behind the surfaces of the news story. "A story is worthless if it doesn't tell me why something happened," says Allan M. Siegal of the *New York Times*. Well, Mr. Siegal goes too far. If we threw out all the stories in the *Times* that failed to answer the question "Why?" there wouldn't be much newspaper left beyond the advertisements. Nonetheless, the why element attempts to make things sensible, coherent, explicable. It satisfies our desire to believe that the world, at least most of the time, is driven by something other than blind chance.

Here is the way the Why impulse—the desire to understand—is communicated in a news story, first in a lead from the *Washington Post*:

> LAS VEGAS—Law enforcement officials on Tuesday continued looking for a motive in one of the deadliest mass shootings in the United States, scouring the gunman's personal and financial history for signals that could help determine what set him off in Las Vegas.

Then by a lead in the *New York Times*:

> LAS VEGAS—Investigators struggled Tuesday with a chilling but baffling array of clues in the wake of the deadliest mass shooting in modern American history as they sought to determine the chain of events that caused a 64-year-old to gun down concertgoers from his hotel suite overlooking the Las Vegas Strip.
>
> "I can't get into the mind of a psychopath," said Joseph Lombardo, the sheriff of the Las Vegas Metropolitan Police Department, on Monday.

Watching one press briefing, I stopped counting how many times experts counseled patience in what they predicted would be a long slog toward the Why.

We live in an age of Why. Some of the questions beg for factual answers: "Why are there so many conflicting models about where Hurricane Ian will make landfall? Why should I evacuate from St. Petersburg two days ahead of time? And, after the storm, why did it take five days to restore power to our street, when many other streets did not lose power at all?"

Perhaps the harder Why questions are the ones about human motivation: "Why do seemingly intelligent citizens deny the effectiveness of vaccines?" "Why did that person who was arrested storm the Capitol?" "Why do some people—during otherwise peaceful protests—destroy property in their own communities?" "Why would a young man, barely out of high school, destroy his own life and the lives of so many others by wielding the power of a semiautomatic weapon?"

Don't fall for the fallacy of the single cause. Good public writing can seek and discover multiple causes for a large event, or the actions of a single individual. Certainty is a false hope: it's a line you can approach, but never cross.

HIGHLIGHTS

- Don't be too quick to publish. Time nourishes good judgment.
- In complex human stories, motive may be something that emerges over time, rather than flashes into sight.
- The answer to the question *Why?* is more reliable when it comes from a variety of sources, rather than a single one.
- Don't be afraid to go back in time to revisit a dramatic human story, even after years or decades.
- Uncertainty or ambiguity is often more human in a story than a clear-cut reason.

32

Lift readers up when they're down.

When it comes to storytelling and public writing, I have devoted myself to serious topics during my career, from literacy to the Holocaust to the AIDS epidemic. When we are overwhelmed by bad news, we often reach for the balm of humor. But the challenge for the public writer is always the issue of decorum, of good taste. If you remember living through 9/11 and its aftermath, public writers began to question the role of irony and satire in our public discourse. It took me months, as I remember, to tell a funny story—about anything.

If I drew up a list of the most popular and productive public writers of the last four decades, high on that list would be Dave Barry (not to be confused with Dan Barry of the *New York Times*, who is also a wonderful writer). Writing for the *Miami Herald*, Dave built an international reputation as a humorist. His syndicated columns, collected in many popular books, spread his name and reputation for cheerful irreverence. (I cannot witness one dog in the park smelling the work of another without thinking of Dave's take that the dog is actually "reading.")

One of Dave's virtues—more important than ever in the digital age—is his versatility. He writes short and long. He has written nonfiction and fiction; he has written for films, television, and audio recordings. Though known for his wit, he often directs it to issues that are deadly serious. His work has earned him many accolades, including a Pulitzer Prize and the Walter Cronkite Award for Excellence in Journalism.

Dave is a good guitar player. On a personal note, I have played music with Dave now and then, once sitting in with the Rock Bottom Remainders, a band of famous authors who are rich and influential enough to pose as rock stars. Actually, they are pretty good and use their celebrity in support of literacy projects. Vocally, Dave favors songs with the names of women in the title such as "Susie Q" and "Gloria." He likes to invent clever names for rock bands.

Early in the pandemic, I began to write the occasional column for the *Tampa Bay Times*, focused on the theme of experiencing the pandemic in the Florida paradise. I would describe these essays as offbeat and whimsical, hitting on such topics as the eccentric ways folks wear their medical masks, such as hanging them over one ear.

In response to that particular column, I received a long message from the daughter of a man who had died in recent weeks from COVID-19. She described how a good laugh on a Sunday morning had lifted her and her mom out of their doldrums. That something I banged out in forty-five minutes could serve as an escape hatch for people who were suffering gave me pause. Maybe we underestimate the role of humor and the offbeat in helping lift folks who feel beaten down.

To help me think this through, I turned to my guru of the goofy, Dave Barry. I explained that I was thinking about what it meant to yuck it up during the years of the plague, and if we needed permission to be funny. Here's what he had to say in our email exchange:

Roy: How has the pandemic and quarantine influenced your own writing? And what have you been working on?

Dave: My son and his family came down from New York and moved in with us, which meant that for four months we had a very full household, including two boys, ages six and one. This had a major influence on my writing in the sense that I was doing a LOT less of it, because I was busy with important grandparent duties such as watching *Moana* 2,317 times.

The kids have gone back to New York, but I'm still having trouble focusing on writing. You'd think it would be easier to focus during the quarantine, since there are so few other things to do, but I've become very skilled at finding distractions. I'll be looking at a blank computer screen, and suddenly I'll think, "I need to change the air conditioner filter RIGHT NOW!"

I've been trying to get started on a novel. I have sort of a half-assed idea for one. All it needs now is a plot. And maybe characters. Also, I wrote a few pandemic-related columns, and have started the Year in Review I do every year. It's always a chore to write, but this year it's going to be a monster. I have already started drinking.

Roy: I remember conversations after 9/11 about whether irony and cynicism were dead, at least for a while. It appears that the culture will allow you to be funny about anything given the passage of time. (I am thinking about Mel Brooks writing "Springtime for Hitler"; and an episode of *Seinfeld* in which they parody the Zapruder film, amateur footage of the assassination of JFK.) After a horrible event, how long should a moratorium on humor last?

Dave: I don't really think there has been a humor moratorium with the pandemic. People have been making jokes about it from the start, because there have been so many surreal elements—the toilet-paper shortage, for example—and because we're all affected by it. I think humor has been keeping us sane.

Roy: Dave, when I think of you, I think, of course, of William Shakespeare. In the play *Macbeth*, right after the slaughter of the king, a character named the Porter delivers a hilarious soliloquy on why too much drinking makes you want to have sex, but messes with your performance. How does the mixing of funny stuff and serious stuff work in your view of the craft?

Dave: At the heart of almost all humor there is some serious truth. The reason we have a sense of humor is that life is scary, and we need some way to deal with our fears, so we turn them into jokes. That is not just my opinion; that's also Shakespeare's opinion. He and I were college roommates.

Roy: In journalism, especially in places like Miami and Florida in general, there is beat reporting and there is offbeat reporting. These days, beat reporting includes global pandemic, economic collapse, social unrest, scary elections. Is there any space left—physical or psychic—for the offbeat and comic? If so, what purpose does it serve?

Dave: I think there are still lots of great offbeat stories out there. The problem is that, as newspapers shrivel, reporters no longer have the freedom to find those stories or the time to write about them. Reporters are under pressure to crank out a lot of short, shallow pieces and hype them on social media. The newspaper business is not what it used to be. And stay off my lawn.

Roy: I am trying to understand what readers get out of humor and satire, especially in a news context. I find that I can't end my day with a news report. I need a rerun of *Seinfeld* or *Married with Children*. Something to sweep away the radioactive waste of bad news. When readers reach out to you, what need do they say you fulfill for them?

Dave: I think readers reach out to me because they know that, when they are finished reading something I wrote, they can be absolutely certain that they will have learned nothing remotely useful. This is reassuring.

Roy: I want to give you a chance to riff on some of your standard comic moves. Have you run into any band names from the lexicon of COVID-19? How about the Mitigators? How about COVID-1965?

Dave: I'm gonna go with Flatten the Curve.

Roy: Your latest book is *Lessons from Lucy: The Simple Joys of an Old, Happy Dog*. It was published before the pandemic hit. If Lucy could talk, rather than howl, what joyful lessons would she teach us to help us survive the moment?

Dave: I don't know if we should look to Lucy for pandemic lessons. She has NOT been practicing social distancing, nor will she wear a mask.

Roy: There are all kinds of writers who may read this. Can you offer three tips for those who might want to experiment with writing humor? (Permit me to go first: Put the funniest word in a sentence at the end, knucklehead.) Your turn, Dave, and thank you.

Dave: That's a good tip. Another one is, don't beat the joke to death—tell it, then move on to the next joke. Be aware that some words are inherently funny: "spatula" and "rectum," for example. Remember that puns are funny only to the punster. And above all, do not neglect to change your air conditioner filter.

There are always some contemporary events in which humor or satire seem impossible. A mass shooting at an elementary school comes to mind. In fact, satire might well be used to call attention to the need for change, holding up to ridicule, perhaps, those who put their gun freedoms above the safety of children. It is no easy achievement and would take a deft touch, an understated outrage. But there are rich historical examples. Perhaps the greatest is *A Modest Proposal* by Jonathan Swift. His acidic critique of British treatment of the Irish includes the "modest" suggestion that the problem of poverty in Catholic Ireland might be mitigated by the poor selling extra babies to the aristocracy as a food source. It hit close enough to home that some Brits thought that Swift, who published it anonymously, was serious.

HIGHLIGHTS

• You don't have to BE funny to WRITE funny. When you read something funny, save it in a journal or computer file. If you QUOTE funny, with attribution of course, the reader will have the same response as if you had invented the joke yourself.

• Shakespeare wrote "The Queen, my lord, is dead," placing the emphatic word at the end. If I were writing a parody of *Macbeth*, I might write: "The Queen, my lord, is sunbathing." In humor, the funny word often goes next to the period.

• Shakespeare was criticized by classical critics for violating certain norms, including the mixing of the comic and the tragic. This "violation" is essential to the genius of the poet, and matches modern sensibilities.

33

Write public stories with a spirit of attention and care.

As we get near the end of this section on storytelling in the public interest, I want to share an example of a whole story and how the elements of narrative work together. These elements include changing the vantage point; using telling details, dialogue, and emphatic word order; employing dramatic tension; raising the stakes; and invoking rituals of death and rebirth. The combination of these strategies creates a special spirit that all public writers should strive for.

As you might imagine, lots of public writers send me good stories to read. The story often comes with a message: "You've got to read this" or "Moved me to tears" or "Best thing I've read in a while." That happened to me in June 2020 during coverage of social protests across the nation and around the world in response to the murder of a Black man, George Floyd, by a police officer. A dear friend, Kelley Benham French, sent me a story written by one of her students, Mary Claire Molloy, a nineteen-year-old first-year student at Indiana University.

The torrent of news of the day—pandemic, recession, civil unrest, mass shootings—inspired her students at IU to step up their game. The story I am sharing here was considered so powerful that it was published first on a local website, The Bloomingtonian, then in the *Indianapolis Star*, and finally in *USA Today*. Because of its impact upon me as a reader and a writer, I am offering Molloy's story in its entirety. Before you read my commentary, make your own decisions about its value. If you appreciate the work—and I think you will—ask yourself "Why?" That is, "What is it about this story that makes it worthy of appreciation? As a public writer, what can I learn from it about the coverage of social justice issues in my community?"

Here is the story without interruption:

A stubborn stain, a selfless act, a wrenching discovery: cleaning up after Chris Beaty's death in Indianapolis

By Mary Claire Molloy

INDIANAPOLIS—He knelt in the back alley, one hand steadying, the other scrubbing. As he worked, the bristles of the plastic brush turned red.

Blood washed down Vermont Street, mingling with a puddle by the yellow curb. The stain left in the alley was stubborn.

It was the stain of two nights of rioting and police confrontation that overshadowed daytime peaceful protests.

It was the stain of one of two killings Saturday night near the protests in Indianapolis, both by bullets. There were flames in Minneapolis, Atlanta, Washington D.C., Los Angeles, New York City. People died in St. Louis, Chicago and here on this patch of concrete downtown.

Ben Jafari didn't know whose blood he was scrubbing, or whether the person was black or white. He knew George Floyd had died at the hands of police officers in Minneapolis, the economy has left millions of people out of work, 100,000 people in the U.S. were dead from COVID-19 and that the country was a tinderbox.

Jafari, who lived a few blocks away, didn't know who was supposed to clean up the mess. On a Sunday morning in a week where it felt like the world was erupting and it was hard to say or do anything to make it better, he figured he could do this much.

"Somebody had to," he said.

A startling discovery

Only later would Jafari learn that the blood had come from Chris Beaty, someone he knew. It didn't matter to him then who it was, he would have done it for anyone.

Jafari, 36, is a real estate developer and the managing partner of the nearby Colonial Apartments. He does not consider himself a political person, but he had marched in the peaceful protest downtown Saturday afternoon. He'd never cleaned up after a death before.

"So, he got shot over there," Jafari said, pointing to Talbott and Vermont streets. He traced the blood, which spread across the alley for at least 40 feet, and gave his best hypothesis.

"Then he ran here, wounded, and must've circled back," he said, eyes following the red splotches as they increased in size. The metallic smell was overpowering.

"He must've died here," Jafari said, pointing to the biggest stain at his feet.

"I really don't know what to say."

An eerie calm the morning after Chris Beaty's death

The Circle City was waking up. The morning sunshine tinted the destruction golden. The shards of shattered windows winked in the light.

Jafari scrubbed.

People, mostly white, were out on Massachusetts Avenue getting their Starbucks fixes and ordering Sunday brunch. A woman, pointing at her menu, said, "Oh, maybe hash browns? Let's do that!"

Graffitied buildings declared, "I can't breathe."

Jafari scrubbed.

Further down on Mass. Ave., a couple held hands with their little boy and little girl, the daughter's pink dress a splash of color against the plywood that covered the windows of a looted Walgreens.

In the alley, a discarded protest sign demanded justice for George, Breonna, Ahmaud, Philando, Sandra.

Jafari was still scrubbing.

"I wipe it down," he said, pouring more ammonia. "But it never goes away."

'I felt like it was my duty to clean it'

Death was not familiar to Jafari. He'd only ever been to a single funeral. He typed "How to clean up blood" into Google. The internet suggested bleach. The grocery store down the street didn't have any. The coronavirus pandemic had depleted the shelves.

The next best and available option was ammonia. Jafari made his way back to the crime scene with two bottles and the plastic brush, along with a broom.

"I felt like it was my duty to clean it," he said. "Out of respect for the victim, out of respect for the city and the people."

He didn't think twice about it, he said. The realization would hit him later—he was cleaning up what had spilled from somebody's son, who nine hours earlier had been alive, right here. It's one thing to see the violence on TV, another to hear it in your own neighborhood, and something else altogether to kneel in someone else's blood.

"George Floyd can't happen again," he said. "We're all just trying to put things back together."

When he gathered his things to go home, the stain was lighter, but still there. He looked down and saw that he'd carried the dead man's blood home with him, on his shoes.

The stain wasn't the blood of a stranger

That Sunday night, he got a text from the property manager at Colonial Apartments. A tenant was missing.

Jafari, lying in bed, read the unit number and knew, right away, who it was.

Chris Beaty was an Indiana University football player and one of the program's most supportive alums. In Indianapolis, he became a well-known business leader and entrepreneur. He and Jafari had attended IU at the same time. Jafari had been to plenty of football games, so he probably saw Beaty play, but they never crossed paths until later. They met at an Indianapolis nightclub and learned how many friends they shared. Beaty had a huge smile and a million friends, and Jafari became one of them.

Whenever they saw each other, they'd greet with a shake up, asking about each other's lives, family, work.

"Hey, what's good, Brother?"

Jafari teared up. The stain he'd been cleaning was not the blood of a stranger, and he could not leave a drop of it in the street.

He set out Monday at 7 a.m.

He returned to the grocery store and bought a heavy-duty brush with thicker bristles. He picked up a bouquet of daisies. He knelt again beside the stubborn stain.

He started to scrub.

The spirit of a story

I am looking for a word that characterizes the effect of this story on me. I could describe the "voice" of the story or the "tone" of the story or the "theme" of the story, but none of those words get there for me. I will choose a word I have never used before in this context. What moves me is the "spirit" of the story.

This story by young Mary Claire Molloy has a spirit. In using that word, I recognize its connection to the word *spiritual.* I am not suggesting that level of significance although there is something compelling and familiar about a man humbling himself—scrubbing bloodstains in an alley—for some higher communal purpose.

The spirit of this story is a spirit of consolation. This selfless action does not compensate for the death of a human being. But in the context of so much suffering, the action of Ben Jafari fills me with hope and courage.

I would go so far as to put this story on a par with a famous precedent by Jimmy Breslin: "Digging JFK Grave Was His Honor" — one of the most influential news columns of the twentieth century. In it, Breslin covers JFK's burial by interviewing the gravedigger. Breslin was a large figure in American journalism, not a college student. And he was covering one of the most significant stories of my lifetime.

What Breslin's story shares with Molloy's is its spirit.

Let's begin with the first two words of Molloy's story: "He knelt." Subject and active verb. Like an ancient heroic poem, this story begins *in media res*, in the middle of things. Stories are forms of transportation, and in a split second we are present next to the kneeling man in the "back alley."

Recognize the distinction between the denotation — the literal meaning — and the connotation of a word. The connotations of a word carry the word's associations, the things that come to mind. "Knelt" connotes prayer, liturgy, reverence, homage, but also subjugation to something or someone more powerful. "Back alley" has dark connotations, places of danger and violence. Think "back-alley abortions." The tension between "knelt" and "back alley" generates a friction that carries through the story.

A report conveys information. It points the reader there. A story is different. It puts us there. One strategy that creates that effect is an appeal to the senses. "As he worked, the bristles of the plastic brush turned red." We can see that, of course, a detail in a movie. But we can hear it as well. The words scrubbing, bristles, and brush all make a sound, an echo of what we would hear if we were on the scene.

Good writers place key words in emphatic locations—often at the end of a sentence, or better yet, the end of a paragraph. Consider the word *red*. This is a story about the act of erasing the red, the color of blood, the symbol of life, transformed into a red stain of death.

We learn that the "Blood washed down Vermont Street, mingling with a puddle by the yellow curb. The stain left in the alley was stubborn." That detail recalls a lesson from my high school English teacher, a priest named Bernard Horst: "Remember that a wall in a story is not always just a wall," he said. "But a symbol need not be a cymbal." That stain is literal, from the blood of a single man. But it is also the blood of the current struggle for racial justice. And it feels like a symbol of a stain that is 400 years old, America's original sin—slavery.

Let's step back to take in the full experience of this story. A good-hearted man, a virtuous citizen, takes upon himself a grisly task, to clean up the bloodstains of a dead man in an alley. He does not know it yet, but the blood is from a man he knows.

This narrative carries with it a sense of ceremony, of public ritual. In an earlier chapter, I shared one theory of public writing that transcends the notion that our job is merely to transmit information. What we experience vicariously here is a kind of ritual, not a janitorial function, but a selfless act of communal grief and hope, like the ancient ritual of carefully preparing the body for the tomb.

We live in the age of the "spoiler alert." When we experience a mystery, we don't want the murderer to be revealed until the end. That impulse is at odds with a news value that requires us to get the key details up high in the report. The headline and story eliminate the element of surprise. But consider this: In the first lines of *Romeo and Juliet*, the audience learns that "a pair of star-cross'd lovers take their life." In the first song of the musical *Hamilton*, Aaron Burr confesses "I'm the damn fool that shot him."

We can learn early "what happened" and still experience the power of "how it happened."

I could teach a semester course on this story. But here are some of the highlights, with specific writing strategies named:

1. See it up close. See it again from a wider camera angle.

> It was the stain of two nights of rioting and police confrontation that overshadowed daytime peaceful protests. It was the stain of one of two killings Saturday night near the protests in Indianapolis, both by bullets. There were flames in Minneapolis, Atlanta, Washington D.C., Los Angeles, New York City. People died in St. Louis, Chicago and here on this patch of concrete downtown.

Think of this move as narrative cartography, a flyover of the nation, with a dramatic return, at the end of the paragraph, to the sacred place. It fulfills its function as a "nut paragraph," revealing the broad news value of the story without losing control of the here and now.

2. *Save the most powerful thought for the shortest sentence.*

> Jafari, who lived a few blocks away, didn't know who was supposed to clean up the mess. On a Sunday morning in a week where it felt like the world was erupting and it was hard to say or do anything to make it better, he figured he could do this much.
>
> "Somebody had to," he said.

This is the first quote in the story, and, because of its brevity, it has the ring of gospel truth. Short sentences as separate paragraphs, swimming in white space, have a special power.

3. *Play the endgame.*

> Jafari, 36, is a real estate developer and the managing partner of the nearby Colonial Apartments. He does not consider himself a political person, but he had marched in the peaceful protest downtown Saturday afternoon. He'd never cleaned up after a death before.

We think of writing in journalism as a front-loaded craft. We tell the news early. But there is also a place in public writing for an ancient rhetorical device: Placing an emphatic word or phrase at the end. In *The Elements of Style*, William Strunk, Jr., argues that the most important places in a written work are the last word in a sentence, the last sentence in a paragraph, the last paragraph in a story.

4. Use dialogue as action.

> "So, he got shot over there," Jafari said, pointing to Talbott and Vermont streets. He traced the blood, which spread across the alley for at least 40 feet, and gave his best hypothesis.
>
> "Then he ran here, wounded, and must've circled back," he said, eyes following the red splotches as they increased in size. The metallic smell was overpowering.
>
> "He must've died here," Jafari said, pointing to the biggest stain at his feet.
>
> "I really don't know what to say."

Let's note the distinction between quotes and dialogue. Quotes tend to halt narrative action. Quotes are about the action. But dialogue *is* the action. Something is happening, and someone is speaking in the midst of action. What we see here is "half-dialogue," one person speaking, but in the presence of another on the scene — the reporter.

5. Slow the pace for emotional effect.

> The Circle City was waking up. The morning sunshine tinted the destruction golden. The shards of shattered windows winked in the light.
>
> Jafari scrubbed.

This begins a passage in which the sentence "Jafari scrubbed" occurs two times, later followed by the variation "Jafari was still scrubbing." That kind of intentional repetition—as opposed to unintended redundancy—sounds like a drumbeat, linking elements together.

This passage moves more slowly than earlier paragraphs. That effect is created by a series of short sentences. The word length of those sentences: 6, 7, 9, 2. Why do I say that the pace is slower? Because each period serves as a stop sign. But why would you want to slow the reader down? I can think of three reasons: clarity, suspense, and, as in this case, emotional impact.

6. Feel the rub.

> Further down on Mass. Ave., a couple held hands with their little boy and little girl, the daughter's pink dress a splash of color against the plywood that covered the windows of a looted Walgreens.

There is a strategy that works in many different creative fields, from music, to the visual arts, to poetry: Put odd and interesting details next to each other. This friction creates heat, which, we hope, creates light. For the poet William Blake, it was expressed in *Songs of Innocence and Experience*. That's what I see here, the little girl's bright dress against the boarded-up background of fear and destruction.

7. Show the talk and the walk.

> "George Floyd can't happen again," he said. "We're all just trying to put things back together."
>
> When he gathered his things to go home, the stain was

> lighter, but still there. He looked down and saw that he'd carried the dead man's blood home with him, on his shoes.

In stories, the words of characters often conflict with their actions. Here Ben Jafari's words may not stand out from those of many other protesters or concerned citizens. His words gain strength from his actions, not eliminating the stain—literal and symbolic—but now carrying it with him. The common shoe stands as an archetype of striving and empathy. We say that we cannot understand another's pain until we walk in their shoes. And we follow in the footsteps of people of virtue.

8. Invoke death and rebirth.

> Whenever they saw each other, they'd greet with a shake up, asking about each other's lives, family, work.
>
> "Hey, what's good, Brother?"
>
> Jafari teared up. The stain he'd been cleaning was not the blood of a stranger, and he could not leave a drop of it in the street.
>
> He set out Monday at 7 a.m.
>
> He returned to the grocery store and bought a heavy-duty brush with thicker bristles. He picked up a bouquet of daisies. He knelt again beside the stubborn stain.
>
> He started to scrub.

It was Shakespeare who predicted that the love poetry of sonnets would make his lover immortal, long after both had passed from this earth. And the Bard was right. Artists of all kinds have the power to bring the dead back to life. It happens here in the briefest exchange between Ben Jafari and Chris Beaty, the only moment when we hear Beaty's voice. He is suddenly alive, not a ghost from the past.

As Mary Claire Molloy reaches for an ending, she returns to two crucial words: "stain" and "scrub." There is the literal meaning that Jafari must work harder with stronger instruments to finish a job. In its symbolism, the passage invites an analogy from mathematics: There is a kind of line on a graph that you can get closer and closer to without ever reaching—to infinity. Maybe it's the same way with the stain that began with slavery: that it takes constant effort and stronger strategies to get to that impossible place where the curve of peace meets the line of justice.

That such excellence in public writing should come from a first-year college student fills me with hope. Mary Claire Molloy had coaching on parts of the story from her teacher Kelley Benham French. She paired her student up with a veteran photojournalist, Jeremy Hogan. It was his instinct to go very early in the morning to the scene of the shooting. Mary Claire's mother drove her there.

When I published an early version of this chapter, I was concerned that my comparison of Molloy's work to that of Jimmy Breslin would seem overstated. Then I received an email from Kevin Breslin, Jimmy's son. He offered that his father would be proud of this young writer.

HIGHLIGHTS

- Public writers don't just make up stories. They report stories. They gather details about characters, develop a sequence of scenes, employ dialogue, present things from a variety of points of view.

- These strategies, as described by Tom Wolfe in his writings about "New Journalism," require more research and reporting, not less.
- When possible, be a fly on the wall. If you can't see events yourself, seek the testimony of eyewitnesses.
- Nonfiction storytellers immerse themselves in the experiences they are writing about, whether in a first-grade classroom where children are learning to read or a tense protest march marred by violence.
- Like ancient poets, you can begin a story *in medias res*—"in the middle of things."
- Look for that detail—that red stain—that signifies the spirit of your story.

34

Write about restoration, not just loss.

I was born in 1948 on the Lower East Side of New York City, a short walk from Chinatown. My first doctor was Doctor Lu. Mom would walk me in a stroller to her favorite Chinese restaurant, where she introduced her baby boy to won-ton soup.

It was with special interest I learned of the devastation that hit the food industry in Chinatown as a result of the pandemic. The problem was more severe than that suffered by restaurants and food workers in other neighborhoods. An ancient and vicious prejudice against Asian people as the carriers of disease, the origins of COVID in China, the images of people in Asia wearing masks—all these ripped the economic heart out of the neighborhood.

More than 300 Asian restaurants turned into 29.

Which is why I was heartened by an August 3, 2022, story on NBC's *Today* show. Reported by Vicky Nguyen, it described the efforts of a young Vietnamese American chef and restaurateur, Helen Nguyen (no relation), to build a coalition to bring Chinatown back. Now 294 food enterprises are open for business.

NBC's story is a good example of what has been called the "restorative narrative."

Public writers, it must be said, pay more attention when something is torn down than when it is built back up. There are plenty of catastrophes to write about. Let's take just one, described by AP reporters, appearing on August 4, 2022:

> A week ago, the scenic Northern California hamlet of Klamath River was home to about 200 people and had a community center, post office and a corner grocery store. Now, after a wildfire raged through the forested region near the Oregon state line, four people are dead and the store is among the few buildings not reduced to ashes.

As a story of breaking news, with climate change made manifest by droughts and wildfires across the West, this report is exceedingly well done. Reporters are brave to even try to get anywhere near a town that has been wiped off the map.

We must wonder, though, whether we will ever hear about Klamath River again. Will we find it back on the map? And how many such firestorms, or floods, or hurricanes, or epidemics, or recessions, or insurrections, or mass shootings must we read about in order to consider ourselves responsible citizens?

This is an old story, as old as it gets. The first stories I remember from the Bible are the loss of paradise, the murder of Abel by his brother Cain, and an angry God destroying the world by flood. As a kid I was kind of disappointed with God for drowning all those animals who could not fit on the ark, and who had done nothing wrong.

Do we see the world as mostly light or mostly dark? Storytellers have a crucial role to play.

The seventeenth-century philosopher Thomas Hobbes may have articulated the darkest picture of human existence, that in a state of nature, without the governing force of a social contract, life would be "solitary, poor, nasty, brutish, and short." (It must be said that Hobbes died in 1679 at the age of ninety-one, so the author of *Leviathan* outlived the "short" part — which is good news.)

Mallary Tenore is an expert on restorative narratives, having served as executive director of Images & Voices of Hope, a nonprofit that gathers and promotes such stories. In an interview with the American Press Institute, she explains what is at stake.

API asked Tenore what we should expect when reporters swoop in to a region or town in the aftermath of a tragedy. She answered:

> It's understandable; they need to be there to inform the public about what happened. But sometimes reporters' approach comes across as insensitive. And after a while,

> these "what happened" stories can make the world feel like a callous place. The persistent focus on death and devastation ignores the fact that there are stories of resilience and recovery to be told.
>
> What, then, we might wonder, is a better approach?
>
> What if, instead of reporting so many "what happened" stories, journalists reported more "what's next" stories that explain how people and communities are finding the strength to move on after experiencing tragedies or other difficult times? What if newsrooms were to put as much emphasis on recovery and restoration as they did on tragedy and devastation?

A consequence of omnipresent negativity is retreat from news and other forms of public information. This experience has been best articulated by journalist and author Amanda Ripley. In a *Washington Post* essay, Ripley explains: "I have a secret. I kept it hidden for longer than I care to admit. It felt unprofessional, vaguely shameful. It wasn't who I wanted to be. But here it is: I've been actively avoiding the news for years."

As a journalist, Ripley covered "terrorist attacks, hurricanes, plane crashes, all manner of human suffering." Each day she would spend hours consuming the news as part of her professional responsibilities. "But half a dozen years ago, something changed," she wrote. "The news started to get under my skin. After my morning reading, I felt so drained that I couldn't write—or do anything creative. I'd listen to *Morning Edition* and feel lethargic, unmotivated, and the day had barely begun." She evolved or devolved from news junkie to news avoider, joining countless fellow citizens who could no longer stand the news.

Ripley is not inviting writers to create uncritical puff pieces or PR jobs. But the truth is that not many stories work without something bad happening at the beginning. Without what Robert McKee calls the "inciting incident," no average New Yorker would stumble upon a corpse at the beginning of an episode of *Law & Order.* Harry Potter would not be orphaned and sleeping under the stairwell. By definition, there can be no restoration without loss.

Ripley's best contribution to this important conversation for writers is to ask what readers need from us, not just as readers or customers, but as members of a community, as human beings. She is specific.

1. "We need hope to get up in the morning."
2. "Humans need a sense of agency.... Feeling like you and your fellow humans can do something—even something small—is how we convert anger into action."
3. "We need dignity." This requires treating people like they matter, listening to them, avoiding the temptation to treat them as the means to a better story.

As I was reading Ripley, I ran into the work of a writer and thinker of an earlier generation, Eleanor Roosevelt. Here was the former First Lady in a 1961 essay in *The Atlantic:*

> There is in most people, at most times, a proneness to give more credence to pleasant news than to unpleasant,

> to hope that, somehow or other, things "will come out all right." But this was not the frame of mind that created the United States and made it not only a great nation but a symbol of a way of life that became the hope of the world. One can fight a danger only when one is armed with solid facts and spurred on by an unwavering faith and determination.

In those last two sentences, Mrs. Roosevelt reaches for two of Ripley's touchstones: hope and agency. The dignity is there in her sensibility and language.

HIGHLIGHTS

- Read *Man's Search for Meaning* by Viktor Frankl, which describes how even during the Holocaust, prisoners of concentration camps looked for ways to find meaning.
- A primary purpose of public writing is to focus attention on significant problems. Not every problem has a solution. But nearly every important problem has someone searching for a solution. Find the searchers and tell their stories.
- Stories exist to show us where the dangers lie, so we can avoid them. But they also show us where the helpers are, so we can find them. Write to reveal the dangers, of course, but also to point to the helpers.
- Remember Amanda Ripley's trinity of readers' needs: hope, agency, and dignity. I will write those three words near my computer as an antidote to becoming too cynical as a citizen and a writer.

• An ancient medieval story about the Holy Grail describes a curse that turns fertile land into the wasteland. The hero must fight and sacrifice and work to restore the land. If you spend all that time on the devastation, please spare some time for the restoration.

• Write stories about the rescuers who help in the aftermath of the disaster. Revisit the ruins after the danger has receded. Chronicle those working to clean things up. Who is the first to rebuild something that has been destroyed? How does it look a year later? Five years later?

Part III

Honesty and Candor

What does it mean to be an honest writer? There are some standard answers, good ones. An honest writer does not steal work from another author. An honest writer does not fabricate characters, scenes, details without letting the reader in on it. An honest writer checks things out, and when things still go wrong, the honest writer corrects mistakes.

But these are basic virtues and actions that should come without much schooling. More complicated — and important for public writers — is how to develop a sense of mission and purpose. As far back as 1913, a great Wisconsin journalism teacher, Willard Bleyer, offered a list of "suggestions" to his students, including these:

- Remember that whatever you write is read by thousands.

- Don't forget that your story or headline helps to influence public opinion.
- Realize that every mistake you make hurts someone.
- Don't try to make cleverness a substitute for truth.
- Sacrifice your position, if need be, rather than your principles.
- See the bright side of life; don't be pessimistic or cynical.
- Stand firmly for what your conscience tells you is right.
- Seek to know the truth and endeavor to make the truth prevail.

These fervent suggestions have relevance more than a century after they appeared at the end of a journalism textbook. They should remind us that craft can be empty without an ethic, a clear sense of duty, something to stand for. It is not enough for that ethic to nag us about what *not* to do. Don't do this, and don't do that. Public writers need a greenlight ethic that inspires them to action, that helps them overcome inhibitions that stand in the way of telling it like it is.

35

Show it like it is.

This book is titled *Tell It Like It Is.* But there are times when we must show it like it is. We can show readers with the visual imagery in our language. In her novel *Arcadia*, Lauren Groff describes a character this way: "In blows an old woman, straight and white, Astrid but smaller, the air around her dense. There is a power to her. A witchiness. Her mouth telegraphs rules, hard chairs, cold-water showers, feline familiars with bladder troubles." What is interesting in that description is not just the concrete language of chairs, showers, and felines — the showing; there is the connection of these things to abstractions, words that describe ideas, like *power* and *witchiness.*

This move from concrete to abstract and back again is

one secret of effective writing, a game we learned in kindergarten: Show AND Tell.

But what do we show, when do we show it, how do we show it, and why?

Those questions now haunt the public and trouble those who serve the common good in both words and images. Public writers and photographers and videographers are beginning to ask whether our communication has been too cautious. Let's take photography as an example (where there are clear parallels to writing).

Were we wrong not to show the public images of dead bodies crushed in the rubble of 9/11? Could the wars in the Middle East be sustained if we were able to see with our eyes the effects of the violence? In the case of mass shootings, would there be a change in the hearts and minds of citizens about gun regulations if they could see the effects of automatic weapons on the bodies of elementary school students? I just watched the testimony of an eleven-year-old Uvalde, Texas, girl who described to authorities how she wiped the blood of her dead classmate on her body and feigned death in order to fool the killer.

These are among the most serious questions we can ask, with no easy answers in sight. Except to say there is a growing appetite for more candor in words and pictures, as long as the efforts are transparent, and as long as the most vulnerable stakeholders are protected.

In an essay for *The Atlantic*, former CNN anchor Brooke Baldwin argues that we should not let the cameras "turn away." She writes:

> Some of the children at Robb Elementary needed to be identified by DNA because their bodies had been ripped apart by assault-style weapons. I remember standing in silence as I watched one tiny white casket wheeled out of a funeral home when I was covering Sandy Hook in 2012. I had the thought then: Would minds change about guns in America if we got permission to show what was left of the children before they were placed in the caskets? Would a grieving parent ever agree to do this? I figured this would never happen. But perhaps now is finally the time to ask.

Critic Tom Jones introduced me to that quote and to the work of Susie Linfield, a journalism teacher at NYU, who in the *New York Times* wondered:

> Photographic images can bring us close to the experience of suffering—and, in particular, to the physical torment that violence creates—in ways that words do not. What does the destruction of a human being, of a human body—frail and vulnerable...look like? What can we know of another's suffering? Is such knowledge forbidden—or, alternately, necessary? And if we obtain it, what then?

The saying that a picture is worth a thousand words is not always true. How many images would it take to compete with the power of the parable of the Good Samaritan or the Gettysburg Address? When images are not available, or when standards and practices will not allow them to be published, or when showing them would offend rather than liberate the mind, the public writer must be ready to step in, to describe with a vivid decorum a moment or scene or image that invites readers to fill in the rest.

Consider a column written by Chris Rose, a reporter in New Orleans describing the destruction he witnessed in 2006 after Hurricane Katrina:

> I drive around and try to figure out those Byzantine markings and symbols that the cops and the National Guard spray-painted on all the houses around here, cryptic communications that tell the story of who or what was or wasn't inside when the floodwater rose to the ceiling.
>
> In some cases, there's no interpretation needed. There's one I pass on St. Roch Avenue in the 8th Ward at least once a week. It says: "1 dead in attic."
>
> ... It's spray-painted there on the front of the house and it probably will remain spray-painted there for weeks, months, maybe years, a perpetual reminder of the untimely passing of a citizen, a resident, a New Orleanian.
>
> One of us.

HIGHLIGHTS

- Readers benefit from both showing and telling.
- The showing helps us see with our senses; the telling helps us understand.
- To show, you need language that we can see, smell, hear, and touch: a bloodstain on the sidewalk, a wad of pink bubblegum stuck on the bottom of a shoe.

• To tell, you need idea words: *intolerance, innocence, fear, aspiration.*

• Learn what your publication considers good taste, decorum, what you might be able to publish in a "family publication." Challenge those standards anytime you are trying to help readers see something painful to reveal wrongdoing or to contribute to public understanding.

36

See it, record it, share it.

To capture difficult moments and to publish them with honesty requires courage, but it does not require you to be a professional journalist, or a journalist of any kind. When I have written here about reporters, editors, or public writers, the emphasis has been on adults who have a professional calling. But the First Amendment ensures that we do not need a license to use the tools of public communicators for the common good.

The years 2020 and 2021 required coverage of the suffering of millions across the globe, and not just because of the pandemic. There were countless stories devoted to the murder of one man, George Floyd, outside a store in Minneapolis called Cup Foods. On May 25, 2020, a seventeen-year-old woman named Darnella Frazier stood on the sidewalk as police officer Derek Chauvin knelt on Floyd's neck for almost ten minutes. She stood there pointing her cell phone at a murder in progress, capturing video that would shock the world and result in Chauvin's conviction on three counts.

Darnella Frazier testified at the trial, explaining how afraid she was when Chauvin reached for his pepper spray, and how she wishes she could have summoned the courage to physically intervene on Floyd's behalf. As Chauvin's convictions were cheered around the world, so was the pluck of a brave young woman pointing a cell phone. She has been showered with praise from President Biden and from celebrities and public figures, such as Michael Moore, Spike Lee, Meryl Streep, Anita Hill, and Senator Cory Booker.

A report on NPR quotes Moore as writing that "No film in our time has been more important than yours." Ann Marie Lipinski, curator of the Nieman Foundation at Harvard, expressed the belief that the video was "one of the most important civil rights documents in a generation."

Such appreciation has led to the question of whether the video should be awarded a Pulitzer Prize.

It would be an unusual prize, to be sure. The material and the creator fall outside the traditional boundaries. At eighteen (seventeen at the time of Floyd's murder), Darnella Frazier would most likely be the youngest winner in history. The prizes in various categories of photojournalism since 1942 have gone to still photographers, not videographers. Frazier was not working for a news organization, acting instead as a concerned citizen within her own community, in the face of a brutal injustice. But there is a good history at the Pulitzers of giving "special citations."

I came to this topic having served as a Pulitzer juror on four occasions — for commentary, feature writing, and twice for nonfiction books. I have one additional vantage point. In 2016 the Pulitzer Prizes marked their centennial. The Poynter Institute, my home base, was one of four institutions to conduct a celebratory gathering and program. The theme of our event in St. Petersburg, which I was honored to lead, derived from Pulitzers won over a hundred years on the topics of social justice and racial equality.

The record of the Pulitzers on these issues — like the record of most American institutions — is a mixed one. In the first decades of the award, women were underrepresented among the winners. The contributions of the Black press were largely ignored, even during the civil rights era. No Black artist was honored until the poet Gwendolyn Brooks in 1950. No individual Black journalist was honored until photojournalist Moneta Sleet, Jr., won "for his photograph of Martin Luther King Jr.'s widow and child, taken at Dr. King's funeral."

That said, our research counted more than a hundred prizes from 1918 to the present that honored work that revealed terrible injustices, held corrupt and racist power accountable, and spoke up, often in the face of physical danger and economic ruin. Many of the earliest such winners were white reporters and editorialists — many from southern news organizations — who spoke up against the terrorism of the Ku Klux Klan. An early example was Grover Cleveland Hall, editor of the *Montgomery Advertiser* in Alabama. Outraged about the flogging of a young Black man at a rural church, Hall led his newspaper on a crusade designed to bring the Klansmen to justice. He exposed Klan members, worked to limit their activities, and supported a law to make it illegal to wear a mask in public.

Progressive white editorialists, such as Ralph McGill and Gene Patterson in Atlanta, rejected any praise for their "courageous stand" against racial injustice. Patterson argued till his dying day that the real heroes were the young Black men and women who put their bodies on the line in protest against American apartheid. He often singled out the late John Lewis, who was the keynote speaker at Poynter's Pulitzer celebration, and who urged public writers to cause "good trouble."

Mention of Lewis should remind us that during the 1950s and '60s, it was often photographic images or film footage of violence against protesters that shocked and enraged Americans at large. Public outrage helped Congress pass landmark civil rights legislation. From Birmingham, I remember footage of peaceful protesters facing firehoses and police dogs. From Selma, we saw Lewis and his colleagues getting their skulls cracked with billy clubs as they tried to march for voting rights. In 1955, a mother published the open casket funeral photo of her lynched and tortured son, fourteen-year-old Emmett Till.

Darnella Frazier's work, I argued in an essay for Harvard's Nieman Foundation for Journalism, lives in that tradition. Her video—almost impossible to watch for its excruciating ten minutes—had a social and ethical purpose, one that aligns with the values of the best public writers and visual communicators:

- To give voice to the voiceless
- To speak truth to power

- To reveal secrets that the corrupt seek to hide
- To stand strong in a moment of personal peril
- To document a fleeting reality that is fraught with meaning

Thinking this through, I called my friend Rev. Kenny Irby, who taught at Poynter for many years before becoming the pastor of the Historic Bethel AME Church in St. Petersburg. He also serves as the director of community intervention and juvenile outreach for the police department. If that were not enough, Rev. Irby happens to be one of America's most influential photojournalists.

When I asked Rev. Irby about the contribution of Darnella Frazier, he invoked the history of street photography and what was once called amateur photography as important complements to the work of professionals. He added the emergence of citizen journalism in the digital age; the evolution from still photography to more and more video; the reality that our smartphones make us all potential photographers. Tomorrow any one of us may find ourselves on the scene in a moment of danger, crisis, or news. The same technology that disseminates TikTok dance videos and cute animals at play gave us the George Floyd video.

I had a concern about my proposal. Is it a healthy thing for such a young person to receive such an honor? Veteran journalists and artists have not always worn such recognition happily. But then I thought of young Swedish environmental activist Greta Thunberg addressing the United Nations. I thought of Malala Yousafzai, the Pakistani girl shot by the Taliban, who at the age of seventeen won the Nobel Peace Prize, the youngest person so honored in any category. I thought of the first National Youth Poet Laureate, Amanda Gorman, and how at twenty-two she electrified the Biden inauguration.

In journalism and other enterprises, we have surely outgrown the generational ladder that required young leaders and creators to wait their turns.

The Pulitzer Prize for Public Service and other categories are often evaluated based on their measurable effects in rooting out corruption and contributing to the public good. That ten-minute video in front of Cup Foods in Minneapolis changed the world. When will we see its like again? Go ahead, I argued in my essay, find a way, give her the prize.

There is always some drama attached to the announcement of awards as prestigious as the Pulitzer Prizes. So it was on that June day in 2021, in the midst of a pandemic, with controversies about racial justice and voting rights aflame, that we learned the news that Darnella Frazier, at the age of eighteen, had received a Pulitzer Special Citation.

Whatever the form of delivery—in print or online, in a podcast, in video, or via still images—the work of citizen journalists has the power to expose corruption and shine a light on noble actions, all in support of the public good.

HIGHLIGHTS

- You don't need a license to serve as a citizen journalist or public writer. But you may need a notebook, a pen, and your cell phone to capture photographs and video.

- When disasters strike—wildfires, hurricanes, blizzards, highway accidents—it is often the "eyewitness to history" who issues the first images or reports.
- This is not a license to become a daredevil, to risk your safety or the safety of others in pursuit of a story. Find a safe place, work with others. Your goal will be to identify a danger to the public good or an important helper for those in need.
- Help us see and understand. The ultimate prize is not a Pulitzer, but the public good.

37

Be clear about where you "stand" as a public writer.

If you have read this far, you already think of yourself as a public writer, or maybe you want to learn how to be one. You have crucial decisions to make in your writing life. What do you want to write — and why? Who do you want to work for? How do you see your personal mission and purpose as someone who is living a life of language?

I remember an old high school cheer: "Lean to the left, lean to the right, stand up, sit down, fight, fight, fight." That was fun when we were in the stands of Lakewood High School cheering for the girls' soccer team. Applied to American politics and culture in the year 2023, that cheer could describe a corrosively divided country. Some of us lean politically to the left, some to the right, and there is a hell of a lot of fighting, with insufficient attention to the common good.

There are those who believe that journalism and public writing should revert to an old tradition of partisanship, that you know when you pick up a publication whether the stories will be chosen and framed from the left or the right. That shift is already happening in some publications and cable television shows. The problem with a partisan view is that it obscures the neutral perspective as a value. There will be many occasions when we need public writers to be neutral, that is, to weigh the evidence of their research without any thought of personal gain or special interest. My goal is not to help you decide whether to lean to the left or right or how far. It is, instead, to help you measure your distance from neutrality and why it matters.

For the purpose of this exploration, I will *not* rely on the word *objective*. It is a good word with a noble history. But it has taken on so many problematic and confusing connotations that it may have lost all practical meaning. I'll replace it with more useful terms. Here are five: *neutral*, *disinterested*, *nonpartisan*, *impartial*, and *independent*. If someone painted a word cloud on the side of an old journalism school, I can imagine these words appearing prominently.

It is in that constellation of words that many but not all journalists and public writers find their duty. The current moment is calling those words—and the standards and practices associated with them—into question. If I am a journalist, or work in any news organization, especially if I am a reporter representing the place, may I march in protest or in support of something, may I donate money to a presidential candidate, may I slap a bumper sticker on my Mustang? May I express my passionately held personal beliefs on social media?

When it comes to issues about "where I stand" as a public writer, I have reached one powerful conclusion: Just because writers choose to be neutral about some things does not require them to be neutral in all things. There will be fervent debates about what those things are.

Public writers need not be neutral about the value of public writing at its best. About the ideals of democracy at their best. About civic participation, especially things such as voting. About the need to improve the quality of education or the environment. To stop the American plague of mass shootings.

In my shop, you could be openly supportive in many ways for human rights and racial justice. But if you are covering the criminal justice beat, you need to write with a level of neutrality about whether we should "defund the police." If you are doing your job, you need to help us understand the various meanings of that phrase, from a variety of points of view.

There are too many variables to count. What kind of organization do you work for? One that aligns itself with a particular ideology? Or one that stands closer to neutrality as a reporting ideal? And within that organization, what is the role of particular writers? What space do they occupy? What genre dominates? Beat reporters, investigators, editorial writers, columnists—all will recognize the freedoms and restrictions that influence their work. That is why each tends to write in a particular voice that represents a discipline within public writing.

Being a writing coach, as I think this through, I find myself asking one particular question again and again: "As you write this, what is your distance from neutrality?" And another: "Where do you want that distance to be?" And another: "How will you create the voice that marks that distance?"

One perspective on these questions comes from Julie Pace, executive editor of the Associated Press, the wire service known traditionally for its neutral reporting.

Here's what Pace had to say to the *New York Times*:

> I understand that sometimes there is an outdated impression of The A.P. or a feeling like we're just a basic wire service putting out choppy sentences. If that is your impression of The A.P., then you haven't been paying attention to The A.P. We produce just incredibly high-level, sophisticated reports across all formats every day.

But what about the A.P.'s distance from neutrality?

> Being a fact-based news organization does not mean that everybody on every side of an issue gets equal hearing, gets equal voice. In certain cases, the facts are just really clear, and we want to make sure that we are amplifying the facts and not muddying the facts. So Covid vaccines are safe. Climate change is real. There was no widespread fraud in the U.S. election. Those are not political positions; those are fact-based positions.

In other words, while the AP remains neutral on many topics and issues, they follow the evidence in support of fact-based conclusions. Neutral on many things does not mean neutral on *every* thing.

HIGHLIGHTS

- To paraphrase media critic Tom Rosenstiel, public writing involves a discipline of verification, not assertion.
- There are too many angry takes in public discourse, designed to grow audiences. Your job is to stay curious, find things out, check things out, and then report them in the public interest.
- Neutrality does not require you to merely report what someone says to you. You can, and should, check it against the available evidence.
- Neutrality does not result from a false equivalency between points of view, one which is strong, the other which is shaky.
- On hot-button issues such as immigration, abortion, and vaccinations, there is no reason to confine yourself to the loudest and most polarized positions. Look for the many in between.
- If you write for an organization, study the standards and practices and interview the veterans to learn what is expected of you.

38

Measure your distance from neutrality.

To help you measure your distance from neutrality, I have created a tool. You can call it an algorithm, a spectrum, a model, or just a measuring stick. It extends from left to right (without the traditional political associations). The higher the number, the farther the distance from neutrality. My standards can be applied to you as an individual writer. Or they can be applied to the organization that publishes your work.

I will differentiate my measuring stick from another scale with a different purpose. There have been reasonable efforts to mark publications that lean to the left or to the right of neutrality on the ideological scale. On such a bias scale, the conservative magazine *National Review* would lean to the right, and, say, *Mother Jones* would lean to the left. On my scale, they would be side by side, exactly the same distance from neutrality.

Here is an overview of my scale, with a fuller description to follow.

1 . . . Neutral . . . 2 . . . Engaged . . . 3 . . . Advocate . . . 4 . . . Partisan . . . 5 . . . Propaganda

In my take, the first four represent different expressions of public writing. Propaganda falls outside the bounds, as it uses the strategies of public writing for purposes that are antagonistic to the public good. Before we describe the responsible stances of public writers, let's tackle propaganda. You will not be writing propaganda, of course, but you need to be the kind of critical thinker and reader who can identify the practices of propagandists. That will help you distinguish good sources of information from bad ones, and, on occasion, fight off vicious lies with a sanitizing truth.

Words change meaning over time. Language scholars call this move a "semantic shift." In the seventeenth century, the word *enthusiasm* had a negative connotation. The etymology from the Greek is "to be inspired or possessed by a god." The word was often applied to religious zealots. In our time, unless we are being ironic, the word can describe a parent cheering at a child's graduation ceremony.

A century ago, the word *propaganda* had an almost neutral meaning. It could be applied to words or images shaped in support of any cause. That was true into the 1940s, when most of the messages produced in the media were in support of the Allied war effort against the Third Reich. An editor who worked at *Life* magazine back then told me that his writers and photographers were loyal propagandists for the USA.

Into and after the war, it was the Nazi propaganda machine that revealed the evil to which lies and disinformation could be put. In subsequent decades the word *propaganda* took what is called a "pejorative" swing, almost always associated now with bad actors and bad intent.

For propagandists, the distance from neutrality is as far as it can be. Fact-checking has no relevance here. Nothing expressed can be justified. It is characterized by disinformation and misinformation; outright lies and fabrications; exaltation of heroes, especially autocrats; demonization of enemies; scapegoating of minorities; disregard for facts and science; hate speech, verging on the criminal; promotion of conspiracy theories; reckless adherence to a demagogue, destructive cause, or profit motive; dependence on repeated slogans; and appeals to baser emotions.

Propagandists and conspiracy theorists often disguise their work to look like legitimate forms of news and public writing. A nickname for this is "pink slime" — a phrase borrowed from the meatpacking industry — in which false information is delivered in packages that look like the news or like reports from authentic professional journals.

Such malpractice can create genuine danger and lead to violence against property and even murder. An eighteen-year-old spent his time on websites that propagated the "Great Replacement" theory, the idea that forces are at work to replace white Christians in America with Black people, immigrants, and Jews. Seduced by conspiracy theories, that man wrote his own racist screed and drove to the city of Buffalo to shoot and kill Black people at a grocery store.

One antidote to the poison of propaganda is the

well-researched neutral report. I wrote this in my book *Murder Your Darlings*:

> When it comes to communication, reports are the building blocks of democratic life. Self-government and responsible enterprise depend on the report. A report differs from a story or an essay or a letter to the editor. To understand how best to write a [neutral] report, consider its opposite: a text that spins or shapes the truth. Subjectivity, partisanship, and bias can never be eliminated from a report, but they can be tamed in the interest of impartiality. There are methods to build reliable reports in every field of endeavor. Pay attention to the connotations as well as to the denotations of words; learn how to unload the language; offer a variety of points of view—not just two; avoid false equivalence. In an era of misinformation, propaganda, and vicious conspiracy theories, we need reports.

What does it mean to be a neutral reporter or writer?

If this is the type of writing you want or need to practice, learn its basic and enduring elements. Neutral writing has no partisan attachment, no connection to a party, union, or other association. It represents no special interest, not a church, not a preservation society, not the Little, Brown publishing company. A neutral writer will declare their independence from outside influences that might be perceived as bias.

A publication that wants to be neutral in its news and information coverage can still express some strong editorial opinions. It's important that these pieces of writing are labeled as opinion. Often readers will detect, fairly or unfairly, bias leaking into the coverage, because of the editorial stance. If you are a neutral writer and accused of bias, do your best to explain that you work for the information side, not the opinion side, of the ship.

Responsible neutral reporters will make mistakes, to be sure, but will correct them with as much prominence as the original error. Not every mistake requires a prominent correction. Misspelling of a common word — no. Misspelling of a proper name — yes.

You may face strict standards against political participation. You can vote, of course, belong to a church, a community chorus, the PTA. But you may be asked not to participate in political protests or to give money to political candidates. Some political journalists have been known for not voting, a form of civic celibacy that is generally perceived as too scrupulous.

Be sure you know your organization's policy on writing for social media. This is encouraged by some, and discouraged by others. If I am writing about City Hall or a pharmaceutical company or a baseball team and trying to appear neutral, the air of neutrality will be dispelled by my sharp opinions on Twitter or Facebook.

Here is a traditional test of neutrality: If I am covering a trial, the reader should not be able to perceive from my report how I might vote as a juror.

HIGHLIGHTS

One of the great champions of the neutral report was the semanticist S. I. Hayakawa, who in 1939 published his now-famous work *Language in Action* (later editions are titled *Language in Thought and Action*) as an antidote to Nazi propaganda. His advice is crucial for all public writers.

- As much as possible, avoid inferences. Don't guess what is going on in other people's minds. This may mean showing rather than telling: not "he was angry" but "he pounded his fist on the table and swore."
- In the neutral mode, avoid judgments, that is, any expression of the writer's approval or disapproval. Not "the senator was defiant," but "the senator's vote was the only one against the bill."
- Exclude words that "snarl," such as "murderous immigrants" or words that "purr," such as "freedom-loving gun owners."
- Avoid judgments and conclusions that "stop thought." By calling a neighborhood "tidy" or "untidy," you keep the reader from having to draw conclusions from specific evidence.
- Discover your bias. Be transparent. Share your concern with an editor, who can help filter out any hint of an unfair slant.

39

Write to be engaged with the community you serve.

This form of journalism and public writing — I am calling it "engaged" — finds paths to public service that do not always require neutrality as a value. What is sometimes thought of as antagonistic to neutral journalism is here reimagined as a positive, such as a belief in the value of diverse points of view on the same experience. It is the direction where many news organizations are leaning, but it lacks a name.

Engagement is characterized by neutral reporting on many issues, but not all; heavy fact-checking, especially upon those in power or with influence; investigations that stand for certain ethical and moral values; editorial positions with labels designed to make opinion transparent; writing in support of civic values such as protection of children, social justice, voter participation, quality education, getting the poison out of the water.

Public writers who are engaged with the community learn to avoid false equivalencies, to weigh and present evidence proportionally. The rules of engagement will not be identical everywhere; they may reflect the values of region, class, or culture. The distance from neutrality here is expressed, often unintentionally, by story selection.

While neutral reporters avoid language that appears "loaded" with opinion, engaged writers may use language that expresses not so much an opinion but a conclusion based on the evidence. They may use words such as *racist* or *lying*. By definition, a journalism of engagement depends not just on a diverse workforce but on expressions of difference and inclusion that do not automatically accept the mainstream white vantage point as the accepted truth.

Wesley Lowery, a journalist known for his work for the *Washington Post*, *60 Minutes*, and other major outlets, has written persuasively on this topic. In the *New York Times* opinion piece "A Reckoning Over Objectivity, Led by Black Journalists," he writes, "The views and inclinations of whiteness are accepted as the objective neutral. When Black and brown reporters and editors challenge those conventions, it's not uncommon for them to be pushed out, reprimanded or robbed of new opportunities."

He argues that "instead of telling hard truths in this polarized environment, America's newsrooms too often deprive their readers of plainly stated facts that could expose reporters to accusations of partiality or imbalance."

Lowery extends his argument into the craft and language of public writing:

> Neutral objectivity trips over itself to find ways to avoid telling the truth. . . . [It] insists we use clunky euphemisms like "officer-involved shooting." Moral clarity, and a faithful adherence to grammar and syntax, would demand we use words that most precisely mean the thing we're trying to communicate: "the police shot someone."

These comments inspired a respectful rejoinder from Tom Rosenstiel, co-author of *The Elements of Journalism*. In a long Twitter sequence, he wrote "I fear a new misunderstanding is taking root in newsrooms today, one that could destroy the already weakened system of journalism on which democracy depends. That misunderstanding is the idea that if we adopt subjectivity to replace a misunderstood concept of objectivity, we will have magically arrived at truth — that anything I am passionate about and believe deeply is a kind of real truth. Wes suggested the term moral clarity as a guiding principle. If that invites people to think that simply opining is some kind of truer or more moral form of reporting, they would be wrong and the effect would be tragic."

I believe that writers can feel energized and not paralyzed negotiating the territory between objectivity and subjectivity, between opinion and information. Somewhere between the "moral clarity" of Lowery and the "discipline of verification" of Rosenstiel rests what I am naming an engaged form of writing. It already exists, and has existed for generations in a variety of publications, often in the form of investigations.

When my wife, Karen, was fifteen years old, she got a job in a chain factory, a company that made costume jewelry, in Providence, Rhode Island. She shouldn't have been working there. It was dirty and grueling work. The *Providence Journal* published a special investigation with this lead sentence: "Jewelry work in Rhode Island is life at the bottom of industrial America."

I see Lowery's moral clarity in that sentence. And after reading the findings, I see the scrupulous application of Rosenstiel's discipline of verification. That lead sentence turns out not to be an opinion or an editorial. It is a responsible conclusion based on overwhelming evidence. The public writers who reported it are fully engaged in the act of rooting out corruption, protecting workers, and serving the public good.

HIGHLIGHTS

- If you don't feel neutral about a topic you are writing about, ask yourself why.
- Make a list of the good things you want your story to accomplish.
- Make another list of the bad things you want to expose.
- Make another list of the key stakeholders, and then check off the most vulnerable.
- Which institutions are responsible for the wrongdoing? Which ones can help to make things right?
- Am I using euphemisms or cloudy language to describe a clear malpractice? What would more candid language look like?

40

Learn the language of advocacy and partisanship.

In our measurement of your distance from neutrality, we have moved from the writer's neutral stance to one that is engaged. Our next steps are toward advocacy and partisanship. *Advocacy* is the word we were left with when the Nazis ripped from the word *propaganda* any of its previous positive connotations. The *American Heritage Dictionary* defines *advocacy journalism* as "journalism in which the writer or the publication expresses a subjective view or promotes a certain cause."

Many if not most public writers are, at one time or another, advocates. Their work is characterized by a story selection in support of a particular cause and interest, such as historic preservation. They pursue a narrower — but deeper — focus on stories of particular interest. They are transparent about their mission and purpose. They don't just cover a cause. They promote actions, including the raising of money, to support a cause. They pay attention to alternative viewpoints — often to debate them.

If you are writing as an advocate, you are likely to cover groups or topics ignored or under-covered by mainstream publishers. You are responsible for fact-checking, most often to target oppositional groups. Accuracy is an essential value, supported by your corrections. To paraphrase the great Aldous Huxley, a good advocate only promotes efforts that are in the "enlightened self-interest" of the public at large.

A partisan works at a further distance from neutrality than an advocate does. As in all these categories, there can be a crossing-over. The *American Heritage Dictionary* defines *partisan* as "a fervent, sometimes militant supporter of a party, cause, faction, person, or idea." While the partisan writer can act — unlike the propagandist — with reason and responsibility, those qualities may be distorted by passionate adherence to the cause.

If you write from a partisan perspective, you create stories, reports, data, and visual imagery used only in support of your cause. They may include personal attacks on opponents, which must be rendered with responsible evidence, not lies and disinformation. You should be accurate, of course, but most of your fact-checking is against the opposition.

Writing from a partisan perspective can be done responsibly but in practice is fraught with ethical dangers. Too many partisan writers characterize opponents in a distorted way (as in political ads). They undermine evidence — including science — if it contradicts their side.

From a language perspective, partisan writing depends too heavily on the repetition of slogans and talking points. Language is loaded to bolster your own cause while denigrating the other's. The partisan writer holds an obvious, but at times unstated, attachment to a political party, church, labor union, or business interest. The only "balance" in coverage is us vs. them. This will be especially evident in the partisan's use of social media.

HIGHLIGHTS

To summarize the key points raised in these chapters about your distance from neutrality, consider these ten questions. How would you answer them? Discuss them with a friend or colleague.

1. Can individuals accurately place themselves along this spectrum from neutral to partisan?
2. Can individuals at strategic moments change their distance from neutrality to become, say, an advocate for a particular cause?
3. What if we were to think of these borders as permeable rather than rigid? Would that help us make practical and ethical decisions about how we write?
4. Could an organization accurately place itself along this spectrum?
5. Could we examine the practices of particular organizations and accurately place them in a category? For example, where might we put *USA Today*, the *New York Times*, *Fox News*, *NPR*, the *Wall Street Journal*?

In your own reading, try to place the work of a particular writer along the spectrum.

6. Could these categories influence the ways in which organizations develop and publish their standards and practices?
7. Could individuals look at these categories and identify the kinds of places they would like to work?
8. Where do powerful social networks stand on this landscape? If they allow publication of *all* kinds of stories, does that make them neutral? Are they a platform or a publisher?
9. How do practices of craft—such as the use of language—create the effects needed to fulfill one or more of these categories? Consider the difference between neutral language and loaded language.
10. If I had to place myself on this spectrum, it would be between neutrality and advocacy. Is *engaged* a useful term to describe that territory? Is there a better one?

41

Write it like it is.

Extraordinary events often produce the best public writing. That was confirmed as I studied the coverage of the attack on the US Capitol on January 6, 2021. For two decades we have had a date stand for a news event. We have 9/11. And now we add January 6.

My book title, remember, comes from one of my favorite songs, sung by the great Aaron Neville: "Tell It Like It Is." That could be the anthem of the moment for journalists and all public writers, along with the lyrics, "Don't be ashamed to let your conscience be your guide." The song played in my head as I read a *Washington Post* story about the attack on the Capitol, written by John Woodrow Cox, based on and incorporating the work of a team of reporters. I know Cox's work from his days at the *Tampa Bay Times*.

In a tweet, Cox shared a four-paragraph lead about what some have called an "attempted coup." He characterized that lead as "the most astonishing four paragraphs I've ever written."

Here they are:

> As President Trump told a sprawling crowd outside the White House that they should never accept defeat, hundreds of his supporters stormed the U.S. Capitol in what amounted to an attempted coup that they hoped would overturn the election he lost. In the chaos, one woman was shot and killed by Capitol Police.
>
> The violent scene—much of it incited by the president's incendiary language—was like none other in modern American history, bringing to a sudden halt the congressional certification of Joe Biden's electoral victory.
>
> With poles bearing blue Trump flags, the mob bashed through Capitol doors and windows, forcing their way past police officers unprepared for the onslaught. Lawmakers were evacuated shortly before an armed standoff at the House chamber's entrance. The woman who was shot by a police officer was rushed to an ambulance, police said, and later died. Canisters of tear gas were fired across the rotunda's white marble floor, and on the steps outside the building, rioters flew Confederate flags.
>
> "USA!" chanted the would-be saboteurs of a 244-year-old democracy.

In linking to that story, Poynter's media writer Tom Jones agreed with Cox, calling the lead "among the most astonishing four paragraphs I've ever read." I think both Cox and Jones are astonished mostly by the events described, amazed that a president would incite an attack on the Capitol. I am astonished by the way the lead was written, and by an epiphany: Language that pushes the boundaries of traditional neutrality can be used in a responsible news report. If you are looking for public writing that is fully engaged, this is it.

Neutral language vs. Telling it like it is

Some may argue that such boundary busting is a bad thing, or at least problematic. We should debate, especially in newsrooms, the language required for telling unvarnished truths, for telling it like it is. Again, I am using the word *neutrality* here rather than *objectivity.* Many of us were raised in a tradition of newswriting in which words like *disinterested* (not having a special interest) or *nonpartisan* guided our choices.

When someone in power spoke and we wrote *said* rather than *admitted* or *conceded* or *boasted*, we were creating a veil of sorts. We wanted to cover the news so that the reader could not detect which side of the issue the journalist was on. The reporter and editor might share a bias, but both had a discipline of verification to guide them to responsible choices.

In recent years, journalists and critics have debated about whether a new social, political, and technological order requires an enlarged set of standards and practices. On CNN's *Reliable Sources* talk show, Jeffrey Goldberg, editor-in-chief of *The Atlantic*, argued for a "commitment to plain language" in moving forward from the attack on the Capitol.

He imagined sentences liberated from traditional constraints. "We have to describe things as they are," he said. What really happened on that terrible day? "The president of the United States incited a mob to go sack the Capitol and lynch the vice president—his vice president." This chapter is not meant as an invitation to abandon neutrality, only to make good choices about when and how to find a necessary distance from it.

In his classic book *Language in Thought and Action*, S. I. Hayakawa wrote about the crucial importance of neutral reporting in the life of a democracy. He argued that such reporting was the antidote to the kind of vicious propaganda promulgated by the Nazis. In one chapter, he argued that reporters should avoid "loaded" language, words that express opinions or draw inferences about whether something is good or bad. And he favored a kind of realistic balance in description, where a good character has some flaws, and a bad one has hidden virtues.

While Hayakawa-style "neutrality" has long been a standard in journalism, it's always been clear that journalists and public writers need not be neutral about everything. They need not be neutral, for example, about violent attacks upon the institutions that make democracy and self-government possible, a system in which they play a crucial role.

Establishing the best distance from neutrality is a task for journalists and those who respect journalism, especially in the aftermath of an administration that propagated attacks on evidence-based enterprises like science and the news industry. I am going to argue that the lead paragraphs written by Cox are neither neutral reporting nor investigative work in which "telling it like it is" is used to shine a light on gross injustice. The language of this lead stands somewhere in between. I have already given it a name: It is the public writing of engagement. The word *engage* has many meanings, some contradictory. But the constellation of denotations and connotations includes ideas of promise, betrothal, agreement, encounter, and readiness for work, as when gears move from neutral to engaged.

There remain in public writing a thousand uses for neutrality. But a neutral frame is often insufficient for the job of revealing the truth in the public interest, for telling it like it is. That's what makes this passage so interesting.

A close look at the craft and standards

Here, then, is my take on these four astonishing paragraphs, paying attention to both craft and standards.

> As President Trump told a sprawling crowd outside the White House that they should never accept defeat, hundreds of his supporters stormed the U.S. Capitol in what amounted to an attempted coup that they hoped would overturn the election he lost. In the chaos, one woman was shot and killed by Capitol Police.

The first sentence is long for a conventional lead—forty-one words. But it is followed by a short one of twelve words, a pattern and rhythm of long/short that many writers find effective.

Keeping it together is an almost invisible chronology:

The president said something, his followers did something, somebody died. It must be said that some critics, friendly to the effort, thought the first word, "As," gave the impression that the speech and attacks were simultaneous, when it would have been more accurate to use a word such as *After.* Intact was the idea of causality.

The order corresponds to key news elements, which the writer must organize for emphasis. It begins with a subordinate clause, not typical of newswriting, but it places Trump's language as less important than the chaos and violence it inspired. The most important news—the attack—is delivered in the main clause. It may feel heartless to say that the loss of life was not as significant as the attack on democratic institutions. That said, the writer finds a dignified position for news of that loss, at the end of the paragraph, an important point of emphasis.

There have been good arguments inside and outside of journalism about what to call the attack on the Capitol and what to call the attackers. Even the words *attack* and *attackers* will be seen as biased to radicals, especially those who might side with those "patriots and freedom fighters" trying to "liberate the people's House."

The verb "storm" has been criticized as romanticizing the action, as in what happens in movies when heroes storm the castle. But it also contains connotations of the Nazi stormtroopers. It seems fair to me.

"Attempted coup" is up for argument, especially among scholars who have studied the different types of actions described by the term *coup d'état*, literally a "blow against the state." Observers and critics have used the word *insurrection*, defined in the *American Heritage Dictionary* as "the act . . . of open revolt against civil authority or a constituted government." That feels closer to what I think I saw.

> The violent scene—much of it incited by the president's incendiary language—was like none other in modern American history, bringing to a sudden halt the congressional certification of Joe Biden's electoral victory.

So much is happening in this second paragraph, a sentence of thirty-three words. It contains four elements of news: 1) a violent scene at the Capitol 2) incited by the president 3) the strangeness of the event 4) the background of the electoral count.

The word "incendiary" is not neutral but, among reasonable people, an expression of cause and effect. The word *riot* is not used here, but its ghost is lurking behind the word "incited."

> With poles bearing blue Trump flags, the mob bashed through Capitol doors and windows, forcing their way past police officers unprepared for the onslaught. Lawmakers were evacuated shortly before an armed standoff at the House chamber's entrance. The woman who was shot by a police officer was rushed to an ambulance, police said, and later died. Canisters of tear gas were fired across the rotunda's white marble floor, and on the steps outside the building, rioters flew Confederate flags.

This third paragraph comprises four sentences filled with sustained action. From a craft perspective, they constitute a kind of narrative, as if the reader were flying over the scene.

Although writers say they prefer verbs in the active voice, this passage proves that the passive can offer its own form of vivid and visual language. A phrase like "the mob bashed through Capitol doors and windows" is as active as you can get. So is "rioters flew Confederate flags."

But look at those places where the subject receives the action: lawmakers "were evacuated"; the woman who was shot "was rushed" to an ambulance, canisters of tear gas "were fired." Active verbs can be vivid, but so can passive ones.

> "USA!" chanted the would-be saboteurs of a 244-year-old democracy.

This is my favorite sentence in the passage, perhaps because of its brevity. It's a narrative sentence with the kind of engagement that comes when two things that are juxtaposed don't really belong together. It may not feel like it, but "USA!" has the same effect as dialogue. The quoted chant transports readers to the spot.

What to call those who attacked the Capitol? They are domestic terrorists, and in particular guises, Trump supporters, white nationalists, neo-Nazis, and so on. The phrase "would-be saboteurs" stands out as distinctive. It's been a long time since I encountered the word *sabotage*, with its French etymology related to the word for "shoe." As I remember it, disgruntled workers might throw shoes into machinery to gum up the works.

How he wrote it, in Cox's own words

That's my take, which is significantly longer than Cox's lead. More than a dozen reporters are credited in support of this story. The ones on the scene, risking their safety to some degree, fed Cox and his colleagues information he used in crafting the entire story. Cox answered my questions about the process.

> **Clark:** You tweeted that your lead was the most "astonishing" thing you had ever written. What astonished you?
>
> **Cox:** The language that the moment demanded: "stormed the U.S. Capitol"; "attempted coup"; "violent scene... like none other in modern American history"; "armed standoff at the House chamber's entrance." This was a work of nonfiction, but here I was, writing those words. And they astonished me.
>
> **Clark:** With a firehose of information coming from so many reporters, how did you decide what to use in the lead?
>
> **Cox:** I'd written quite a bit, pre-publication, when it suddenly became clear early in the afternoon that our story needed to focus on the Capitol riot, which meant I had to start from scratch. I've anchored maybe three dozen "lede-alls," as we call them, since I came to the *Post*. [A "lede-all" or "lead-all" is an introduction that offers an overview of events.] My boss, Lynda Robinson, has edited nearly every one. We've developed a great rhythm, often under intense pressure, and we needed it Wednesday. We decided right away that it needed to open

with a line that married Trump's words at the White House with the attack at the Capitol.

Then I took a couple deep breaths and started to sift through the stream of short, frantic feeds coming in. I had a sense of the sweep I wanted to deliver, so what I was looking for were specific, compelling details—the sort that would let me zoom the camera all the way in.

Clark: I define news judgment as deciding on behalf of the reader what is most interesting and most important. How did you sort out the news elements and how to stack them in your lead?

Cox: The structure of the top came to me almost immediately, which I'm thankful for because it often doesn't go that way.

I think of endings as destinations, and I like to write toward them, so after we settled on the first paragraph, I focused on the fourth. In this case, "USA" being chanted by a group of violent insurrectionists ravaging the citadel of American democracy had to be the concluding beat of that opening thought. It wasn't the nut graph, in the way we traditionally define them, but it was the essence of the story I hoped we would deliver. [A "nut graph" or "nut paragraph" tends to appear in the third or fourth paragraph and explains to readers why the story is important.]

The second paragraph needed to tell, not show. We had to put this event into historical context, while tacking on the news that the riot had stopped the election's certification.

I wanted a robust third paragraph loaded with arresting detail that would set up the absurdity and horror of the fourth. By then, I didn't have time to go back through the feeds, so I went with what stuck out in my memory. Years ago, when I was a police reporter at the *Tampa Bay Times* and on a tight daily deadline for a narrative, an editor told me to put down my notebook (until fact-checking, of course) and write what I remembered. The best material would surface in my mind. It was great advice, and I think the best material surfaced again Wednesday: the bashing through doors, the armed standoff, the woman shot, the tear gas on the Rotunda's white marble. The words "Confederate flags" had to come last to create that juxtaposition with the next word: "USA."

Clark: It feels as if you were blending reported information with some storytelling. That third paragraph has lots of narrative action. How do you think about the mix of information and story elements?

Cox: I want everything I write to read like a story, not an article. Scene, dialogue, tension, a kicker [ending] worth waiting for. I do my best to thread the obligatory information into those elements rather than taking big pauses that could halt the momentum. It helps, of course, when you're taking feeds from such a talented group of reporters who can spin together textured vignettes under pressure.

Clark: Anything else you think other public writers would be interested in?

Cox: I wrote this story, sure, but there's a reason my byline came last — and if we were allowed to add a dozen more bylines, it still would have come last. My colleagues risked their lives to tell the world what was happening.

That's not hyperbole. A member of the maskless mob surrounding them carved "MURDER THE MEDIA" into a door. But they were undeterred. I've never been prouder to be a journalist or to work at the *Post* than I was that day.

HIGHLIGHTS

The voice of the writer is a kind of illusion. We hear it, even when it is coming to us off the page or the screen rather than in our ears. That voice is created by the sum of all the strategies used by the writer to create the effect of speaking directly to the reader. So what are those effects? They are in the analysis above, but here is a list for your workbench:

- As you gather information, either on your own or from others, begin to imagine the shape of the story, especially what you need for an effective beginning and a good ending.
- Try not to panic in the face of unusual pressures. Follow your process, especially when it comes to your lead or introduction.
- Ask the basic questions: What really happened? What is my focus? What do readers need to know?
- When writing about actions that endanger the common good, avoid hazy language, equivocations, or false balance. Be candid. Write it straight.
- If you are writing about an event that is spread out over time and space, use the "lead-all," three or four paragraphs that offer an overview.

- If you begin the story with an anecdote or an overview, a good tool to follow is the "nut" paragraph, a section that pins down the news or the focus.
- You can mix information with narrative elements, such as quick scenes, dialogue, and sharp, telling details, such as the Confederate flags clashing with the chants of "USA."

42

Consider when an untruth becomes a lie.

Let's return to that classic distinction discussed among many writers, the one between showing and telling. Some say "show, don't tell," but that should be considered a preference, not a rule. If you are like me, sometimes we show, sometimes we tell, and sometimes we do both.

Political arguments often evolve (or devolve) into debates about language. Pro-choice vs. Pro-life. Illegal aliens vs. Undocumented workers. Traitors vs. Patriots. I remember a debate about whether events in the Middle East should be described as a civil war or sectarian violence. When asked my opinion, I suggested that the writer could never go wrong by describing, as accurately as possible, what was happening on the ground.

There are long-standing inhibitions about naming the thing. These come from standards of reporting that push the writer away from loading the language and supposedly slanting the story. If there is vandalism against a synagogue, the reporter will describe the swastika graffiti on the wall with language quoting Hitler. Is it then necessary to refer to the person as an antisemite? Can we describe the acts of racists or sexists in terms of their actions and consequences without calling them that? More and more, reporters are finding a way, as well as the need for achieving distance from neutral language. They are calling a lie a lie, and a big lie a big lie.

Let's take as an example a text from Calvin Woodward, published by the AP in May 2021, at a time when elements within the Republican Party continued to declare that the election of President Joe Biden was fraudulent or illegitimate. I discovered the text via a tweet by media critic and scholar Jay Rosen. He admired the text for its candor, but argued that it "Took a LONG time for the press to get here — too long" to call a lie a lie.

While the AP is known for establishing a standard for nonpartisan reporting, it is clear from this text that it has lowered the barriers to "telling it like it is." For years, public writers had tried to "write around" the word *lie*. A politician could say things that were not accurate, or that could not be verified, or that others called into doubt, or even that were untruthful. But a "lie"?

A lie as bold and corrosive as a stolen presidential election strikes at the heart of the legitimacy and integrity of the democratic process. What is needed is a vigorous defense of the facts, linked to a strong condemnation of cynical untruths—or should I call them lies?

It is worth a closer look at the language of this form of engaged public reporting and writing. Here are sections of Woodward's text with my commentary:

> WASHINGTON (AP)—Allegiance to a lie has become a test of loyalty to Donald Trump and a means of self-preservation for Republicans.

I would be hard-pressed to find a twenty-word lead to a report that does as much work as this one. It is constructed upon three phrases that are almost parallel: allegiance to a lie; a test of loyalty; a means of self-preservation. I have often argued that three is the largest number in writing because it gives the feel of a completed statement: of the people, by the people, for the people. Another way of describing this has to do with the sharpness of the focus. There is no hedging here at the top, no attribution yet, no sourcing, just a clear declaration of what the evidence shows.

> Trump's discredited allegations about a stolen election did nothing to save his presidency when courtrooms high and low, state governments and ultimately Congress—meeting in the chaos of an insurrection powered by his grievances—affirmed the legitimacy of his defeat and the honesty of the process that led to it.

This fifty-word paragraph does what all such texts do: It supports the lead and builds a defense of the use of the word "lie." It flashes back and then offers a kind of aerial view of past prevarications, with phrases such as "discredited allegations" and "chaos of an insurrection," which bump into the counterbalancing forces of verification: "affirmed the legitimacy" and "honesty of the process."

> Now those "Big Lie" allegations, no closer to true than before, are getting a second, howling wind.

The story reveals that the phrase "Big Lie," used to describe Trump's false claims about a stolen election, has been appropriated by the disgraced former president to challenge the validity of Biden's election. But "no closer to true than before" maintains the rigorous discipline of verification. Most interesting is "getting a second, howling wind." It's a mixed metaphor of a sort. To get a second wind means to pick up speed and energy after a period of tiring out. But "howling" can refer to the force and sound of the wind, or the insufferable screech of a howling windbag.

> Republicans are expected to believe the falsehoods, pretend they do or at bare minimum not let it be known that they don't. State Republican leaders from Georgia to Arizona have been flamed by Trump or his followers for standing against the lies.
>
> Only a select few Republicans in Washington are defying him, for they, too, know that doing so comes with a cost.

Another efficient passage. The AP rejects the Oxford comma, which would make the three elements clearer and more balanced as in "believe the falsehoods, pretend they do, or... not let it be known that they don't."

Such a news treatment would not have been possible, I believe, had it not been for the emergence of a global movement to scrupulously fact-check the words, ideas, and opinions of those in power.

HIGHLIGHTS

- The *American Heritage Dictionary* defines the verb *lie* this way: "To present false information with the intention of deceiving." The public writer may fact-check a statement and find it inaccurate. That does not make it a lie. A lie is an intentional act of deceiving. And a big lie has great consequences.
- Use of the word *lie* should be reserved for special cases when the evidence is overwhelming and the stakes are high.
- I would not use these moral descriptors (*liar*, *racist*, *antisemite*) without conversations with colleagues, editors, and other stakeholders.
- When in doubt, show in vivid terms what is happening on the ground, as the *Washington Post* team did in its coverage of the attack on the Capitol. Readers will draw their own conclusions.

43

Debunk misinformation without calling more attention to it.

I want to lend my support to an experiment on how to solve a serious reporting problem for all public writers. Important people tell lies. Journalists seek to expose those lies and the bad intentions behind them. The exposure of a lie can spread the lie. Do I ignore the lie and hope it does not become poison in the body politic? Do I report it, check it against the facts, and leave it to the public to render judgment?

Or is there another way?

I am late to the game, but my tardiness has now let me examine the opinions of journalists, scholars, and critics Jay Rosen, Yamiche Alcindor, George Lakoff, Brian Stelter, and Margaret Sullivan. The proposed antidote to political lying even has a name, which I first heard on the CNN show *Reliable Sources* with Brian Stelter: the "truth sandwich."

It derives from the work of George Lakoff, an expert on strategic language and the framing of civic arguments. His proposed formula, summarized on Twitter, goes like this:

> Truth Sandwich:
>
> 1. Start with the truth. The first frame gets the advantage.
> 2. Indicate the lie. Avoid amplifying the specific language if possible.
> 3. Return to the truth. Always repeat truths more than lies.

Jay Rosen, a north star among academic critics of the news media, tweets: "Some lies and acts of disinformation are too important to be ignored. But repeating them in news accounts only helps them spread. What to do? Position the troublesome claim between true statements, like a sandwich."

Rosen cites a tweet by Yamiche Alcindor: "It's been a few days since VP nominee Kamala Harris joined Joe Biden's ticket & birtherism attacks have begun....a Trump campaign advisor is openly questioning whether Harris is eligible to be on the ticket. Harris was born in the United States & is clearly eligible."

Rosen's reading of Alcindor's tweet: "First state what is true. Then introduce the truthless or misleading statement. Then repeat what is true, so that the falsehood is neither the first impression nor the takeaway."

My modest contribution to this idea comes from the world of practical rhetoric, used in journalism and literature. But before I get there, I can't resist tweaking the name of the strategy. Critics of Lakoff are way ahead of me. A column in the *Wall Street Journal* by Crispin Sartwell argues that Lakoff's solution to manipulating the people is to find a different way to manipulate the people. The headline: **'Truth Sandwich'? Baloney!**

Let's think about the phrase "truth sandwich" for a minute. By turning a report into a sandwich, I have turned the reporter into a short-order cook. This appeals to me in a New York City tabloid, working-stiff kind of way. The reader is hungry. I serve up something tasty. What kind of sandwich do you want? Ham and cheese? Tuna? BLT? Whatever the reader orders, the stuff that defines the sandwich goes in the *middle*. So, in a sense, Yamiche Alcindor has not served up a "truth" sandwich, but a "lie" sandwich. The lie is in the middle. The bread provides the pieces of truth to contain the lie. Tweaking the *WSJ*: Truth on the outside. Baloney in the middle.

In a rhetorical sense, we can refer to this as "emphatic word order." This strategy is so important in all of public writing that I list it as number two among my fifty-five top writing tools: "Order words for emphasis. Place strong words at the beginning and at the end." My favorite example comes from the tragedy *Macbeth*. There is a scream offstage. A messenger enters and announces to the ambitious Thane of Cawdor: "The Queen, my lord, is dead." As my students and colleagues know, I never tire of parsing these six words. I would have written it "The Queen is dead, my lord." But Shakespeare is up to something in his version. He uses two commas, which invites the actor to slow his delivery for dramatic effect. The Queen is so important that she comes first, the subject of the sentence. The courtly etiquette, "my lord," not essential to our basic meaning, is tucked in the middle. The news, the nut, the tragic epiphany — "is dead" — comes last, where it resonates.

The shape of that — very important, not so important, even more important — bears the structural elements of our proposed sandwich. Emphatic sentence order!

In the necrology of the news craft — the language of death — traditionalists might accuse Shakespeare of "burying the lead." Of course, to place the most important element first would make the actor sound like Yoda: "Dead the Queen is, my lord."

In spite of the top-heaviness of news stories, journalists have their way of honoring a good ending, usually in the form of a "kicker" — a clever send-off.

What I am saying here is that public writers understand *positioning as a form of emphasis* — even news judgment. The most common editorial gesture is to take something from down in the story and move it up, giving it greater attention. The second most common gesture is to take something less important and move it down in the story.

The position of least emphasis turns out to be the middle. As the great journalist Jacqui Banaszynski once confessed to me: "I have been praised for my leads. I have been praised for my endings. But I have not once been praised for my middles." It is possible to emphasize something in the middle with the reward of a sparkling quote or a revealing anecdote. This works best when it illustrates a point at the top and leads to what will come at the bottom. But if that central point is so interesting or so important, you may not want it hiding in the middle.

We think that forms of news telling and public writing have existed forever. The truth is that they were all created — the wire service report, the human-interest story, and now the tweet — to solve new problems and to serve new markets. In all cases I can think of, technology preceded ethics, which can take a long time to catch up.

The main lesson here is that word order and sentence order are crucial to creating meaning. They are strategies that are used promiscuously by liars and conspiracy theorists. Those of us who want to tell it like is — with clarity and honesty — must demonstrate how to use these strategies to tell the truth and debunk lies in the public interest. Let's get cooking.

HIGHLIGHTS

- Do your best not to republish lies and disinformation, even if your goal is to expose them.
- One way is to offer information in a 1-2-1 structure: tell the truth, expose the lie, tell the truth.
- Any word or phrase that comes at the end of a sentence will get special attention, whether you want it to or not.

- During revision, take notice of the ends of sentences and paragraphs to make sure that your best material is not hiding in the middle.
- You can emphasize something in the middle, but only if story elements lead to and then lead from that scene or revelation.

44

Write with integrity in the plain style.

I know how to tell you the truth in a sentence so dense and complicated and filled with jargon that you will not be able to comprehend it. I also know how—using my clearest and most engaging prose—to tell you a vicious lie. This dual reality—that seemingly virtuous plainness can be used for ill intent—lies at the heart of the ethics and practice of public writing.

The author who revealed this problem most persuasively was a scholar named Hugh Kenner, and he introduced it most cogently in an essay titled "The Politics of the Plain Style." Originally published in the *New York Times Book Review* in 1985, Kenner included it with sixty-three other essays in his book *Mazes.*

When I began reading the essay, I thought it would

confirm my long-standing bias that in a democracy, the plain style is most worthy, especially when used by public writers in the public interest. A good case can be made for the civic virtues of the plain style, but Kenner, in a sophisticated argument, persuaded me that some fleas come with the dog.

A disappointing truth is that an undecorated, straightforward writing style is a favorite of liars, including liars in high places. Make that liars, propagandists, and conspiracy theorists. We have had enough of those in the twenty-first century to make citing examples unnecessary. And the last thing I want to do is republish pernicious texts, even for the purpose of condemning them.

When rank-and-file citizens receive messages written in the high style — full of fancy effects and abstractions — their "bullshit detectors" kick in. That nice term, often attributed to Hemingway (who actually said "The most essential gift for a good writer is a built-in, shock-proof shit-detector"), describes a form of skepticism that many of us need to sense when we are being fooled or lied to.

If I tell it to you straight, you will look me in the eye and pat me on the back, a person of the people, one of you. Literary styles and standards shift with the centuries, including the lines between fiction and nonfiction. Among the so-called liars cited by Kenner are famous authors such as Daniel Defoe and George Orwell. Both, he argues, wrote fiction that posed as nonfiction. The way Defoe persuaded us that Robinson Crusoe actually lived, or that Orwell actually shot an elephant and witnessed a hanging, was to write it straight. That is, to make it sound truthful.

If public writers are to embrace a plain style in an honest way, they must understand what makes it work. Kenner argues:

- That the plain style is a style, even though it reads as plain, undecorated
- That it is a contrivance, an artifice, something made up to create a particular effect
- That it exists in ambiguity, being the perfect form of transmission for democratic practices, but also for fictions, fabrications, and hoaxes
- That it makes writers sound truthful, even when they are not

If you aspire to write in an honest, plain style, what are its central components? Let's give Kenner the floor:

> Plain style is a populist style.... Homely diction [common language] is its hallmark, also one-two-three syntax [subject, verb, object], the show of candor and the artifice of seeming to be grounded outside language in what is called fact—the domain where a condemned man can be observed as he silently avoids a puddle and your prose will report the observation and no one will doubt it.

Kenner alludes here to Orwell's essay in which he watches a hanging and observes the oddity of the condemned man not wanting to get his feet wet as he prepares to climb the steps to the gallows. "Such prose simulates the words anyone who was there and awake might later have spoken spontaneously. On a written page, as we've seen, the spontaneous can only be a contrivance."

He adds:

> The plain style feigns a candid observer. Such is its great advantage for persuading. From behind its mask of calm candor, the writer with political intentions can appeal, in seeming disinterest, to people whose pride is their no-nonsense connoisseurship of fact. And such is the trickiness of language that he may find he must deceive them to enlighten them. Whether Orwell ever witnessed a hanging or not, we're in no doubt what he means us to think of the custom.

Orwell has been a literary hero of mine from the time I read *Animal Farm* as a child. I jumped from his overt fiction, such as *1984*, to his essays on politics and language, paying only occasional attention to his nonfiction books and narrative essays. I always assumed that Orwell shot an elephant and that he witnessed a hanging, because, well, I wanted to believe it and assumed a social contract between writer and reader, that if a writer of nonfiction writes a scene in which two brothers are arguing in a restaurant, then it was not two sisters laughing in a discotheque. As to whether Orwell wrote from experience in these cases, I can't be sure, but he always admitted that he wrote from a political motive, through which he might justify what is sometimes called poetic license.

Writing to reach a "higher truth," of course, is part of a literary and religious tradition that goes back centuries. When Christian authors of an earlier age wrote the life and death stories of the saints—hagiography—they cared less about the literal truth of the story than a kind of allegorical truth: That the martyrdom of St. Agnes of Rome was an echo of the suffering of Jesus on the cross, and therefore a pathway to eternal life. I write this as a lifelong Catholic, without disrespect or irony. Such writing is a form of propaganda and is where we get that word: a propagation of the faith.

Orwell's faith was in democratic institutions, threatened in the twentieth century by tyrannies of the Right and the Left—fascism and communism. Seeing British imperialism as a corruption, he felt a moral obligation to tell stories in which that system looked bad, including one where, as a member of the imperial police in Burma, he found himself having to kill an elephant, an act he came to regret. Using the plain style, Orwell makes his essay so real that I believe it. In my professional life, I have argued against this idea of the "higher truth," which does not respect fact, knowing how slippery that fact can be.

Now that we are in the digital age, a writer's fabrications—even those made with good intent—are often easily exposed, leading to a loss of authority and credibility that can injure a worthy cause. With Holocaust deniers abounding, why would you fabricate a story about the Holocaust when there are still so many factual stories to tell?

There is a powerful lesson here for all public writers: That if I can imagine a strong plot and compelling characters, I do not have to fabricate a story and sell it as nonfiction. I can write it as a novel and sell it as a screenplay! I have yet to hear an argument that *Sophie's Choice* is unworthy because it was imagined rather than reported. I am saying that *all* forms of writing and communication fall potentially under the rubric of public writing. That includes fiction, poetry, film, even music lyrics, labeled as such: "Tell it like it is," says the song, "Don't be ashamed to let your conscience be your guide."

In the end, we need reports we can trust, and even in the age of disinformation and fake news, those are best delivered in the plain style—with honesty as its backbone. Writing in the plain style is a strategy; civic clarity and credibility are the effects.

HIGHLIGHTS

When you are writing reports, when you want your audience to comprehend, write in the plain style—a kind of middle ground between an ornate high style and a low style that gravitates toward slang.

- The plain style requires exacting work. Plain does not mean simple. Prefer the straightforward over the technical: shorter words, sentences, paragraphs at the points of greatest complexity.
- Keep subjects and verbs in the main clause together. Put the main clause first.
- More common words work better.
- Easy on the literary effects; use only the most transparent metaphors, nothing that stops the reader and calls attention to itself.
- Remember 1-2-3 syntax, subject-verb-object: "Public writers prefer the plain style."

45

Check facts in the public interest.

Among its other activities as a resource for journalists and public writers, the Poynter Institute, my home base for many years, has become the center for a global network of fact-checkers. PolitiFact, a website published originally by the *Tampa Bay Times*, won a Pulitzer Prize and offered a different paradigm on how politics might be covered, especially in the heat of election cycles.

Rather than just cover the horse race and offer competing claims by candidates, a team of journalists compares those claims and purported facts against the available evidence. A public figure's claims would earn one of six grades: True, Mostly True, Half True, Mostly False, False, and the ignominious "Pants on Fire," emphasized with the image of a blazing gauge, a so-called truth-o-meter. A popular feature is the "Lie of the Year." It—the lie—seems to get bigger with each passing year.

When the pandemic hit early in 2020, it required fact-checkers to divide their attention between traditional political issues and concerns related to science and public health. Add a troubled economy, climate crises, and social unrest, and the team was plenty busy. I was delighted to see them tackle the issues raised by COVID head-on. An essay by my colleague Daniel Funke offered such a useful set of observations about public writing that I knew I would be sharing them here.

With the collaboration of the PolitiFact team, I offer these tested strategies and concerns that might help anyone writing about public health, at any level, do a better job. With the gracious permission of Funke and his editors, I am paraphrasing his findings, combining his words and conclusions with some clarifying language of my own:

1. Speculation thrives in the unknown.

In science, there is always more to know. The best you can do is keep gaining on certainty and adjust public policy when appropriate. In spring 2020, there was a lot that scientists didn't know about the coronavirus, including where it came from, how it spread, or how to treat it.

Those uncertainties left a gap in public knowledge about the virus and the disease it caused, COVID-19. Misinformation, especially on social media about fake cures, filled that gap. We know much more now, but the dissemination of bad information will not stop. Remain skeptical of any claims on social media or elsewhere that seem to lack context about the virus. Most important, especially if you are a public writer: Don't share something on social media unless you know it's true.

Before you are able to tell us that something is true, you may be able to tell us that something is *not true*.

2. Denying reality has broad appeal.

From the earliest days of the pandemic, there was a concerted effort by politicians and commentators to deny or downplay the severity of COVID-19.

Pundits likened the coronavirus to the common cold (False) and the flu (Pants on Fire). Politicians selectively cited data to make the virus seem less deadly than it actually was. On social media, some denied the existence of COVID-19 altogether or posted photos of empty hospital beds to claim the crisis was fake.

Of course, the crisis was real. "When people are fearful, they seek information to reduce uncertainty," said Jeff Hancock, a communications professor at Stanford University. "This can lead people to believe information that may be wrong or deceptive because it helps make them feel better, or allows them to place blame about what's happening."

3. People wearing white lab coats can be good disinformers.

During the pandemic, millions of people saw a video that claimed face masks don't work, that the coronavirus was manipulated, and that the drug hydroxychloroquine was an effective way to treat it. The messenger was a discredited scientist, but a source with the air of authority. Add a white coat and a slick video, and millions of viewers are led down a dangerous path.

Some of the most persuasive coronavirus misinformation comes from people who appear to know what they're talking about. Just because someone wears a lab coat and has a medical degree does not mean their claims about COVID-19 are accurate. Get your facts from public health agencies with good track records to avoid being duped.

4. Conspiracy theories overlap.

What do anti-vaccine advocates, right-wing conspiracy theorists, and lockdown protesters have in common? In 2020, they all teamed up to spread conspiracy theories about COVID-19. Microsoft co-founder Bill Gates was a common target, falsely accused of planting microchips in people via vaccines. The glue that holds these disparate conspiracy forces together, of course, is social media. "These networks are wired to spread disinformation about the virus," said Kate Starbird, an associate professor at the University of Washington.

5. Falsehoods can flow from the top down.

When you think of online misinformation, you may think of social media rumors, conspiracy theorists, or foreign disinformation campaigns. But in 2020, a lot of coronavirus misinformation came from the White House.

In February 2020, Trump told the country to view the

coronavirus "the same as the flu," a line echoed by pundits and Facebook users throughout the year. He promoted a drug as a potential coronavirus treatment, setting the stage for others to claim the drug was a miracle cure. In the weeks leading up to Election Day, Trump falsely claimed the United States was padding COVID-19 death numbers.

Sometimes, the president would repeat misinformation he saw online. At many other times he himself was the source of much of the coronavirus misinformation. It illustrates how those with the biggest platforms have the biggest potential to misinform.

You would think that most of the misinformation in a pandemic would come from the "bottom up," to use a phrase by professor of government Brendan Nyhan. It becomes a much more difficult problem when it flows from the top down, hits the bottom, and comes bubbling back up.

6. Misinformation has consequences.

According to Funke, "False COVID-19 claims are more than just a distraction from the public health crisis—they can directly affect people's lives and health." He cites as an example a Florida taxi driver and his wife who got sick after believing the conspiracy theory that medical face masks were somehow connected to 5G data networks. The wife later died from complications of COVID-19. Nurses and doctors on the front line of the pandemic took to social media to dispel rumors, some of which they heard from patients who were sick with COVID-19.

The effect of misinformation can also be seen in polling

data from 2020. One poll from December showed that 40 percent of Americans believed the coronavirus was created in a lab in China.

Other reports are less discouraging. While conspiracies have spread, the number of believers in those conspiracies has remained stable. Disinformation did not stop more than 70 percent of Americans polled from expressing a willingness to take the vaccines that could protect their lives and the lives of their loved ones.

HIGHLIGHTS

- If you are a public writer, you should tap into responsible fact-checking networks such as PolitiFact. It's a good first step in telling it like it is.
- Understand the difference between doctors and scientists who make mistakes or who work from limited data and those bad actors who wear white coats to disinform in their own ideological or financial interests.
- When debunking misinformation, do your best not to call too much attention to the lie, or to repeat the language of the lie. Good fact-checkers have a way of drowning a lie with truth. Check out the clever formulation called the "truth sandwich."
- When you hear the leader of an organization misinform, know that the people who know best what the leader is doing are those who work for him or her. Some are collaborators, but some are willing to help journalists and other public writers understand the motives and methods of the disinformers.

- Anytime you are on social media, check the batteries on your B.S. detector and make sure it is switched on. Turn the dial somewhere between skepticism and cynicism.
- Public writers have no responsibility to "balance" a verifiable fact with an alternate one.

46

See things anew as a conceptual writer.

During a time in which I have written extensively about the method and mission of public writers, it is hard to think of a writer with a more public profile than Nikole Hannah-Jones. It is no exaggeration to call her one of the most honored and controversial journalists of the last decade. We may need to go back to Woodward and Bernstein for examples of newspaper journalists with a higher profile.

I have had the opportunity to teach with Hannah-Jones on two occasions at the Poynter Institute, so I've studied her work and watched her in action. Of the thousands of words devoted to her, I feel there is one area of interest that is undernourished. It is not the Five *W*s; it's the *H*: *how* she does what she does.

The great Canadian journalism scholar and teacher

Stuart Adam argued that the best journalism excels in four areas: news judgment, reporting and evidence, language and narrative, and analysis and interpretation. It is in this last category—the ability to see meaning in the midst of seemingly disconnected patterns, to re-imagine, re-vise, re-frame, and re-name—that Hannah-Jones demands our attention. She can do what is called shoe-leather reporting, and she has the conceptual ability to see the larger framework. It's a rare combination.

Her recent honors include a Pulitzer Prize and a MacArthur Fellowship, commonly referred to as a Genius Grant. Controversy accompanied her application for a tenured professorship at her alma mater, the University of North Carolina (UNC), and one group of historians challenged the evidence in her influential work on race, *The 1619 Project*. That continuing project, which now includes books and school curricula, has led to accusations, mostly from the right, that Hannah-Jones's work is part of an effort to inject what is sloppily labeled "critical race theory" into public education at every level and that she is not producing journalism but "woke propaganda."

Spurred on by state legislators, parents have approached school boards to purge libraries and classrooms of reading material they find objectionable—especially material on race, gender, and antisemitism. Some banned works, written by winners of Pulitzer or Nobel prizes, have difficult, at times disturbing, themes. That is their point. Curious students will seek them out—especially if they are banned. That's me in the corner of the Williston Park Public Library on Long Island at the age of thirteen sitting in a dusty corner reading *The Naked and the Dead*. The irony is that every banned book I can think of becomes more notorious, and thus more popular, because of the efforts to ban it. (School board members: Please ban this book!)

Some of the criticism directed at Nikole Hannah-Jones came from an influential Arkansas publisher, Walter Hussman, Jr., who donated $25 million to UNC, and who believes that the standards of journalism should elevate "impartiality" above all other values. The result was that the university withheld a tenured professorship from Hannah-Jones, then offered it under a cloud of national scandal and threat of a lawsuit. Ultimately, Hannah-Jones rejected that position and set up shop as the tenured Knight Chair in Race and Journalism at Howard University, developing a program in journalism and democracy.

Her story is an important one to practitioners of public writing everywhere. It raises questions for both individuals and organizations: What do we stand for? On what issues should we be impartial? What controversies demand our direct engagement? What strategies of thinking, reporting, storytelling, and writing lead us to the most useful version of the world — and of our history — in the public interest?

The cultural issues and arguments have eclipsed something just as important: a single strategy that allows writers of good faith to achieve a distance from neutrality. In history, it is sometimes referred to as revisionism. In journalism and public writing, it has a clever name: the "conceptual scoop."

Hannah-Jones expresses herself as an engaged, conceptual public writer of the highest order in *1619*. That work is a sweeping historical concept that calls itself "A New Origin Story." Rather than think of the birth of the nation as being sealed in 1776 or 1789, what if we thought of it as occurring in the year 1619, when the *White Lion*, the first ship carrying enslaved people from Africa, landed in Virginia? The story of the ship that arrived a year later, the *Mayflower*, gave us the narrative that people from England came to a new world to obtain religious freedom. It is that story that was turned into a national myth that over the centuries became celebrated on one of our most sacred civic holidays.

The 1619 Project invites us to regain the lost parts of our history, to revise our stories about our founding mothers and fathers, to stare in the face the truth that the highest ideals of American liberty and democratic government failed to respect and protect the descendants of those first enslaved people. There were many white people with abolitionist beliefs who took violent action against slavery. It took a civil war. It took race riots after World War I. It took Supreme Court decisions that sparked resistance. It took what we now think of as the civil rights movement in the 1950s and '60s. It is taking new forms of protest in the wake of police killings of Black people. Hannah-Jones's conclusion is that it took the courage and militancy of Black people to lead America, now over centuries, to what Lincoln called "our better angels," toward the perfection of our ideals. In a key essay she quotes the great W. E. B. Du Bois: "Would America have been America without her Negro people?"

In "Arrival," an essay in the book *Four Hundred Souls*, Hannah-Jones responds to that question:

> We cannot fathom it. Black Americans, by definition, are an amalgamated people. Our bodies form the genetic

> code—we are African, Native, and European—that made America and Americans. We are the living manifestation of the physical, cultural, and ideological merger of the peoples who landed on those ships but a year apart, and of those people who were already here at arrival. Despite the way we have been taught these histories, these stories do not march side by side or in parallel but are inherently intertwined, inseparable. The time for subordinating one of these histories to another has long passed. We must remember the *White Lion* along with the *Mayflower*, and the Powhatan along with the English at Jamestown. As Du Bois implores: "Nations reel and stagger on their way; they make hideous mistakes; they commit frightful wrongs; they do great and beautiful things. And shall we not best guide humanity by telling the truth about all this, so far as the truth is ascertainable?"
>
> The true story of America begins here, in 1619. This is our story. We must not flinch.

Walter Hussman, Jr., considered by many an innovator and astute businessman, has devoted his energy and resources to the strengthening of local news. But he objected to Hannah-Jones's journalism, especially to the thesis at the heart of *1619*, that "For the most part, Black Americans fought back alone."

Here is Hussman:

> I think this claim denigrates the courageous efforts of many white Americans to address the sin of slavery and the racial injustices that resulted after the Civil War....

> Long before Nikole Hannah-Jones won her Pulitzer Prize, courageous white southerners risking their lives standing up for the rights of blacks were winning Pulitzer prizes, too.

Hussman has made it clear that his objection to *1619* rests not just in its particular thesis but in that it has a thesis at all. It represents a paradigm of journalism that will hurt the credibility and viability of all journalists, he argues. He takes his stand here, on the sharp point of neutrality and impartiality, a credo he wants young journalists to see every day and come to believe in.

Anyone who had conducted a thorough review of Hannah-Jones's writing over the length of her career would find many works that would be judged "impartial" by any fair observer. There reaches a moment in an investigation, though, when traditional reporting is necessary but insufficient to reveal an important truth. Enter the conceptual scoop, described in a 1996 essay by Paul Starobin:

> Conceptual journalists are more interested in figuring things out than in finding things out—their impulse is to explain, to interpret, to move from the particular fact to the general proposition. What they do is no substitute for shoe-leather or what-happened-yesterday stories. But it can help people make sense of the torrent of raw data.... And the focus of conceptual journalists on political ideas and culture is particularly well suited for an era of crumbling paradigms about the role of government....

> But more skeptical journalists point out that a snazzy conceptual take can camouflage a multitude of sins, including slack reporting and embedded bias, and serve the dubious function of packaging old ideas in shiny new wrappers.

Few stories require the conceptual range offered by Hannah-Jones in *1619*. Let me break down the process for one of the simplest genres of conceptual writing, the "trend story." A cynical newsroom thought is that if you can find three examples of something, you have a trend, but, in a pinch, two is enough. To notice a trend, you have to be paying attention. Perhaps while bingeing on Netflix, you notice how many dystopian dramas people are watching during the pandemic. Or you are walking around the park and notice more and more people playing the paddle game pickleball. Or you hear three neighbors say they have seen coyotes nearby, usually at dusk.

I have lived in St. Petersburg since 1977. Back then it was satirized as one gigantic old-folks home, but not anymore. I was driving around the other day and noticed how many coffee shops and breweries had opened in the downtown district. Tom Brokaw called the people who fought World War II the "Greatest Generation," which is a broad version of a conceptual scoop. On certain days, I think that the millennials are the greatest generation because they have given us more and better coffee and beer, whenever we want it, wherever we want it. Welcome to "St. Petersbrew."

That last move is a common one for the more conceptual writer: to give a new name to an insight, a trend, a set of connections, a rising movement. In politics, it has been expressed in phrases that describe voter blocs as "soccer moms" or

"NASCAR dads" or "Volvo Republicans." It need not be a catchy phrase. It can be a number: *1619.* To do her duty as a teller of truth, Nikole Hannah-Jones decided that while journalists could be neutral about many things, they should not be neutral about everything.

Certain factions of journalism are leaning her way. They are establishing the distance from neutrality that best exemplifies their sense of mission and purpose. While their reports and narratives are not neutral, I would argue that they are not advocacy, partisan, or propaganda. They are finding a place between reporter and advocate, a space I have characterized as a "journalism of engagement."

That makes it sound as if Hannah-Jones is leading a movement, and maybe it will come to that someday. There are movements in journalism: the human-interest story; investigative work; New Journalism; computer-assisted reporting; public or civic journalism; and others. They do require a point person—sometimes more than one. They can be guided by a transparent manifesto that reveals standards and practices. And they benefit from an anthology, a set of "mentor texts" as high school teachers describe them, that others can learn from and emulate.

HIGHLIGHTS

Here are some ways to become a more conceptual public writer:

- Do your homework, your research. Learn the details. Walk the beat.

- Pay close attention to the world you cover, whether it's your house or the state house.
- Travel along different routes, the main streets, the side streets, the alleyways.
- Safely and politely approach strangers: If you notice something different, ask them what they are doing. Watch for patterns.
- Talk to experts: If you see more murals around town, talk to a muralist.
- Discuss the pattern you see with friends and colleagues to test your notion that something is afoot.
- In a memo to yourself, try to describe what you are experiencing.
- Summarize it in a short paragraph, a short sentence.
- Give it a name.
- To build your conceptual muscles, leverage your continuing education. Whatever your field of study—science, anthropology, history, economics, political science, literature—you will find meaning in the events of the world.

47

Learn the best practices of science writers.

Since this section is about honesty and candor, I dare to write this solemn truth: The most maligned mark of punctuation among journalists and public writers is the semicolon. They fear it, avoid it, doubt their ability to use it correctly. It seems stodgy, archaic, and academic, traits they are determined to avoid. Instead, they use the dash—promiscuously.

But the semicolon has its fans. I am one of them. I devote a chapter to it in my book *The Glamour of Grammar*, in which I offer the metaphor of the "swinging gate": "That's how I see the semicolon in my own writing, as a gate that stands between two thoughts, a barrier that forces separation but invites you to pass through to the other side."

To appreciate the semicolon, we need to see it in action. I

remember the morning I was introduced to the writer Ed Yong. Of all those covering the story of the coronavirus, according to my colleague Tom Jones, one writer stood above the rest. Jones wrote:

> *The Atlantic*'s Ed Yong has been a rock star — an absolute must-read throughout this pandemic. And his latest story for *The Atlantic* is nothing short of elite. His richly reported analysis — "How the Pandemic Defeated America" — elicits every negative emotion, from sadness to frustration to helplessness to outright seeing-red anger.

He then highlights one of Yong's paragraphs for our close attention:

> No one should be shocked that a liar who has made almost 20,000 false or misleading claims during his presidency would lie about whether the U.S. had the pandemic under control; that a racist who gave birth to birtherism would do little to stop a virus that was disproportionately killing Black people; that a xenophobe who presided over the creation of new immigrant-detention centers would order meatpacking plants with a substantial immigrant workforce to remain open; that a cruel man devoid of empathy would fail to calm fearful citizens; that a narcissist who cannot stand to be upstaged would refuse to tap the deep well of experts at his disposal; that a scion of nepotism would hand control of a shadow coronavirus task force to his unqualified son-in-law; that an armchair polymath would claim to have a "natural ability" at medicine and

> display it by wondering out loud about the curative potential of injecting disinfectant; that an egotist incapable of admitting failure would try to distract from his greatest one by blaming China, defunding the WHO, and promoting miracle drugs; or that a president who has been shielded by his party from any shred of accountability would say, when asked about the lack of testing, "I don't take any responsibility at all."

Jones describes this as a paragraph, which it is; but, more remarkable, it's a sentence, a single sentence of 212 words. No journalism text I know of would recommend such a length. But Yong makes it work with a little help from his language friends. They are placement of subject and verb, the word *that* used as a subordinating conjunction, and, of course, the semicolon. Not just one semicolon, mind you, but eight. In one sentence.

One of the secrets to crafting such a sentence is to make sure that the subject and verb of the main clause come early. If meaning is created in the first few words, the writer is free to stretch out with examples. Yong sets the stage with five one-syllable words: "No one should be shocked..."

What follows is one of the most useful and underappreciated words in the English language: *that*. That word appears ten times in the sentence. It begins the litany of subordinate clauses. It marks the drumbeat of parallel constructions. And because it is just *that*, it is hardly visible. Because you can barely see it, *that* lacks the power to hold the big pieces together. A cathedral sentence such as this one requires the equivalent of flying buttresses to support its weight. The framework that separates the parts, but also holds them together, is created by our modest friend the semicolon.

If Yong has written the sentence of the year, and I believe he has, he can thank the semicolon; we all can. I wonder whether Yong thanked his friend the semicolon in 2021 upon receiving the Pulitzer Prize for explanatory reporting, the first Pulitzer ever won by *The Atlantic.*

Beat writing in the public interest

Like a world war, a global pandemic is too big a story to be covered by any one beat. Think of the public writers who cover science and medicine, education, business and the economy, transportation, entertainment, the environment, government and politics at every level, criminal justice and social inequality, and, yes, sports. These are traditional and common areas of coverage that all have been energized by COVID and its consequences. This is a crucial lesson for any writer covering a specialized area: In the end, you cannot cover your specialty well if that is all that you are covering. You must follow the ripples in the pond.

Here's what Yong told the Poynter Institute's Stephen Buckley on the scope of the pandemic story in 2021:

> This is an omni-crisis. It truly is huge in scope, in its stakes. It touches on every sector of society so, while I am a science journalist who's written about pandemics before, this is clearly not just a science story. It's also an education story, a politics story, a culture story. It

> transcends beats and it transcends areas of expertise, which makes it very challenging to cover.

From that same interview, Yong offers advice for public writers covering science, or any technical area:

On uncertainty:

> If we do our jobs correctly, we should be well-geared towards running at uncertainty and embracing uncertainty, rather than shying away from it or being cowed by it.

On writing during a period of denialism about science:

> I've described the process of covering COVID-19 as like being gaslighted on a daily basis by absolutely everyone, from some random person on Twitter to the president of the United States. And that is an ongoing battle that just erodes at your soul.

[Derived from the title of a 1944 film, the word *gaslight* denotes being fooled over a period of time into doubting your own experiences and believing an alternative reality. —RPC]

On the mission of public writing during something like a pandemic:

> Compare the pandemic to a raging torrent, a body of water that moves at high speed and threatens to sweep us all away and drown us in this sea of information and also

misinformation. I think of good journalism as a platform in the middle of that, something for people to stand on so that they can observe this torrential flow of history moving past them without themselves getting submerged in it. And that's the kind of mindset that I tried to bear in mind throughout 2020 and the kind of purpose that I was trying to instill in the work that I was doing.

On the pace of news vs. the pace of science:

For any topic that I write about, I try and talk to a range of different people, get a range of different views from experts who might well disagree with each other, and then present that to readers. I see that as a strength rather than a weakness, and the more complicated, the more divisive, the more controversial something is, the more people will then be reaching out to comment. I try very hard to integrate across all those different lines of expertise to come to my own conclusions, but then also to showcase that range of opinions to people.

On the rejection of science:

This actually doesn't feel like that enormous a mystery to me. It's very consistent with everything we know about the science of science communication, which is a huge and very interesting field in itself. It fits with everything we know about climate denialism, about anti-vaccination attitudes, which primarily is this: That you can't displace feelings with facts.

That's a horrible thing for journalists to hear, because we're in the business of offering people facts. But people aren't empty vessels into which you pour information. People process information through the lens of their own personal identity, through their political identities, through what their communities are saying, through their sense of belonging with their friends and their families. Anything that we write and any information that we give is always going to be passed through the filter of those identities and those sorts of cultural values.

All the strategies that Ed Yong describes as applying to the writing about pandemics applies to climate catastrophes. In both cases, the ability of scientists and science writers to persuade may be inhibited by some of their most traditional values and practices. Alice Bell makes the case in her book *Our Biggest Experiment: An Epic History of the Climate Crisis*. She writes:

> We are now living our ancestors' nightmares, and it didn't have to be this way. If we are looking to apportion blame, it is those who deliberately peddled doubt that should be first in line. But it is also worth looking at the cultures of scientific work that have developed over centuries, some of which could do with an update. The doubt-mongers manipulated positive forces in science—such as scepticism—for their own ends, but they also made use of other resources, exacerbating generational divides, exploiting the scientific community's tendency to avoid drama, and steering notions about who were

> legitimate political partners (e.g., governments) and who were not (activists).
>
> Scientists working on climate change have been put in an incredibly difficult position. They should have been given time, expert support and a decent budget to think about the multiple challenges and transformations that happen when you take a contentious bit of science out of the scientific community and put it in the public sphere. They should have been given that support from government, but they also needed the gatekeepers within the scientific community to help them, too. And yet, if anything, many of these scientists have been ridiculed by their colleagues for speaking to media or—perish the thought—showing emotion.

The intentional suppression of emotion by public writers—in the name of some professional detachment—can be a counterproductive inhibition. It can prevent the writer from telling it like it is.

HIGHLIGHTS

- During tumultuous times, think of your writing as a safe spot from where your reader can view the swirling currents around you.
- Cover your specialty, of course, but realize that you cannot tell the full truth or extract the meanings that matter most without making connections outside your specialty.
- If you need examples, consider how a pandemic affects everything from education to employment to sports.

- No field of study, even science, achieves certainty. A creative uncertainty is always a part of the process of learning, which means you must share with your readers not just what you know but also what you do not yet know.
- Help readers understand that the pace of public information is a lot quicker than the pace of knowledge. Science research takes time; learning in the classroom takes time; climate change, by definition, takes time. This may require you to visit and then revisit a topic again and again.
- Expressing emotion—in science or in public writing—may be necessary to tell it like it is. You can read that emotion in Yong's takedown of Donald Trump.
- Oh, yes, honor the semicolon; think of it as a "swinging gate."

48

Teach the next generation of public writers.

Most authors have some idea — or at least a hope — as to who will read their books. I have learned, especially since the publication of *Writing Tools*, that this conception can be way off, at times in a good way. Many more kinds of writers than I had imagined have reached out to me with testimonials about how that book helped them in their work. It is gratifying for an author.

My hope is that *Tell It Like It Is* will be read by public writers of all persuasions, from the young freelancer to the seasoned professional. My further hope is that it will be read in classrooms. Let's create a nation of public writers. To get there, we must create college and professional classes and curricula devoted to writing in the public interest.

One of the most important lessons I ever learned from language experts is embedded in the phrase "discourse community." In my translation, it is a "language club." All of us belong to several — probably dozens.

I am a musician. An English literature scholar, who favors Chaucer and Shakespeare. A journalist. A writing teacher. An author. A Floridian, by way of New York, Rhode Island, and Montgomery, Alabama. I have Italian relatives — and Jewish ones. I am a father and husband and brother. For more than a decade, I coached girls' soccer teams. I love basketball and baseball. I have watched pro wrestling since I was a little boy. I am a white male of a certain age. I use computers and my cell phone — a lot. My oldest daughter describes herself as queer and is married to a transgender person. I have watched television almost every single day of my life since 1948. I belong to all of these language clubs, some of which are broad, others fairly narrow. I can shift from one dialect to another. In a way, I am multilingual.

A university comprises a rich number of discourse communities, each marked, at the highest level of accomplishment, by the acquisition of a technical language that others outside the club find it difficult or impossible to understand. Some call that technical language jargon, but not me. *Jargon* has taken on negative connotations, delivered mostly by critics who do not belong to the club. "There is no reason to speak or write that way," runs the typical line, "except to keep knowledge to themselves and to make them appear smarter than they really are." When we stand outside the club, it is easy for us to dismiss the discourse inside it.

Imagine that my publisher has given me enough money

to create my own university. It will have courses and programs in all the usual academic disciplines. Here are some of them:

Health and Medicine
Hard Sciences
Political Science and Law
Education
Business and Economics
Math and Computer Science
Social Sciences
History
The Arts
Philosophy and Ethics
Language and Literature

It is crucial, I would argue, that students graduate from a program with a strong knowledge of its technical language and with the ability to communicate with others in that field. It has been years since I taught a class on *The Canterbury Tales*, but I'll wager I could read a new edition of the *Chaucer Review*, in which I was once published, and make my way through it with some level of understanding.

Let's call that proficiency a disciplinary literacy.

Like the Midas touch, this knowledge has some unintended side effects. One of them is an inability or unwillingness to communicate with others outside the club. *Epistemology* is a funny word that I learned as an undergraduate in a philosophy class. I once said that I did not know "piss from epistemology," but I was lying. I have the ability to flip the switch.

To move from a narrow language club to a much broader one. Just as I translated "discourse community" into "language club," so I can translate *epistemology* into "the study of how we know things, and, beyond that, how we know what we think we know." That's deep, but now accessible, because I am using not my philosopher voice but my *public voice*.

Through the Poynter Institute, I have been consulted as a writing coach by the World Bank, IBM, AAA, the AARP, the United Nations, and the US Department of Health and Human Services. (I was greeted there by the leader of a department whose title on her business card was twenty-six words long. She welcomed me to the place "where language goes to die.") I have worked with the Stetson University College of Law. I have consulted with the National Oceanic and Atmospheric Administration (NOAA) and was once called upon by the CDC. When I asked the good folks at NOAA why their writing was so dense, they said they would like to write more clearly but that two forces prevented it: scientists and lawyers.

In all these cases, leaders worried about the inability of their communications team to write purposefully for a large public audience in comprehensible, interesting prose. There are many reasons people get panicky when it comes to an epidemic like, say, AIDS or Ebola. There are many reasons that millions doubt global warming is a problem made worse by human beings. There are many reasons some parents refuse to vaccinate their children.

At such crisis points we need experts in biomedical or environmental science disciplines who have professional authority AND the ability to communicate in a strong, persuasive public voice, liberated from jargon, liberated from the inhibition that they are just "dumbing things down." No, professor, you are not dumbing it down, you are making the strange familiar—and for the public good.

At my university, every student in every discipline would graduate as "bilingual," possessing the ability to communicate in their own discipline and then to serve a much larger audience in a *public voice.* The capstone project would be writing a thousand-word essay that might appear in a magazine or on an editorial page. You would have to defend that essay in front of an audience of civilians and scholars.

Which brings us to this question: Who at my university would teach public writing? I can attest that the English departments or composition programs at many—but not all—colleges have the capacity. There are also some good education programs where aspiring language arts teachers are taught to teach reading and writing by professors who use the common language in a responsible way. At Vanderbilt University I have collaborated with, under the leadership of historian Paul Kramer, a group of scholars who meet, work on their own writing, and take that knowledge of craft into the classroom.

You may disagree, but I think the discipline that produces work that most resembles public writing is journalism. There are sub-disciplines such as advertising, marketing, speech writing, and strategic communication. They all draw their strength, I would argue, from journalism as a discipline. Journalism, wrote my Canadian colleague Stuart Adam, is "the democratic craft."

The more abstract disciplines have traditionally looked down upon journalism and its cousins. But that condescension is proof of the need for reform. Let's learn from our colleagues in all disciplines who try to help their students communicate in a public voice. Let's work together.

49

Share the spirit of good writing.

As a child, one of my favorite Bible stories was about the Tower of Babel. It comes from the book of Genesis and is an ancient myth told in many religions and cultures. It concerns the time after Noah's Flood, when human beings repopulated the world and rebuilt civilization. As they got stronger and stronger and prouder and prouder, they aspired to be more godlike and built a great structure that would reach the heavens.

As someone attached to the Judeo-Christian tradition, I think it's fair for me to write that the God of the early scriptures can come off as a bit vindictive. First, he casts Adam and Eve out of the Garden, then he drowns any creature not on the Ark, and then he destroys the tower and curses human beings with a confusion of languages. What do we get out of it? The word *babble*. In a clever turn, a company named Babbel sells language-learning products.

About fifty days after Easter, Christian churches celebrate the Feast of Pentecost (*Pentecost* means "fiftieth day"). As a Catholic boy I was fascinated by the celebration—one of the only days when priests wore red vestments—and by the story that comes down to us from the Acts of the Apostles. The followers of Jesus, who are now without their leader, are gathered in a room in Jerusalem for a religious observance that attracts pilgrims from many nations.

Something amazing happens. The disciples hear a great wind, and tongues of fire descend upon them, filling them with the Holy Spirit. This gift, one that Jesus promised them, inspires them with courage and the power of language. The next day, Peter, not known as an orator, tells the story of Jesus to a great multitude, and they are amazed. Even though they come from many places with many languages, everyone in the crowd can understand him.

It is perceived as a miracle, and one does not need be a biblical scholar to see that Pentecost is the antidote to Babel. Instead of confusion of language, humans get to hear the "good news" in a harmony of languages. Public writing at its best.

I am retelling these stories not to evangelize but to draw energy and inspiration for all of us who consider ourselves public writers. In the American tradition, some of the most important expressions of public language come from the rabbi in the temple and the pastor in the pulpit. While we think of them as serving certain communities of believers, their influence extends beyond the walls of their holy places. Consider the reach of preachers and teachers throughout history, from Jonathan Edwards to the Rev. Martin Luther King, Jr.—from "Sinners in the Hands of an Angry God" to "I Have a Dream."

We know that the words of the anointed and self-anointed, including some notorious televangelists, can be venal and vicious, which is why selfless and virtuous speech must be celebrated wherever we can find it. In that spirit, I want to share what I see in that journey from Babel to Pentecost.

A superficial moral of Babel is that human beings should know their place and not make God angry. Or to borrow a lesson from the great Jim Croce: "You don't tug on Superman's cape; you don't spit into the wind; you don't pull the mask off that old Lone Ranger; and you don't mess around with"...Him.

What if we framed the story as not one of overweening pride and loss, but of the way in which humble and steady work can lead to the reconciliation of differences? God has given human beings a problem to solve: how to come together and make meaning with language.

Writing across difference is one of the great challenges and opportunities of the current age. At a time when citizens contend about the nature of science, the verifiability of facts, even the meaning of words, public writers have a big job on their hands, and on their tongues. Limited by our own biases, by our own cultures and experiences, public writers need intense periods of listening and learning.

Good public writing requires what has been called not the golden but the platinum rule. In the first, we treat a person the way *we* would like to be treated. In the second we treat a person the way *they* would like to be treated. We can't know that without asking, listening, interacting, and then writing in the public interest.

Which brings us back to Pentecost. The word *spirit*, as in "the Holy Spirit," comes from the Latin word for "breath." Someone who expires is dead. If you are inspired, it means something has gotten into you, perhaps a talent or a gift — of writing or speaking or understanding or learning — that helps you do your job and reach others in a special way.

So many people who write all the time tell me, "I'm not a writer." There is a lot of evidence that the fisherman named Peter was not a great intellect or orator. His failures are the stuff of history. Yet something got into him one day in Jerusalem, and without invitation he faced a multitude, spoke his truth, told it like it was. And the people were amazed.

50

Keep reading to perfect your craft.

It should be obvious that if I want to be a sonneteer, I need to read more sonnets. The aspiring chef will eat delicious food prepared by the master. The architect will visit cathedrals. We make things and must learn how they are well made.

If you have read *Tell It Like It Is*, you know that you can't stop reading now. So many books, so little time. Here is a list of books that have influenced my work and that will help you grow in your craft. I am presenting them to you in a strategic order, as a syllabus, of sorts, for public writers.

Let's begin with *Language in Thought and Action* by the great semanticist S. I. Hayakawa. Written in response to Nazi propaganda, it offers a path to a critical and creative use of language. It honors the report as a tool of democracy and introduces us to the "ladder of abstraction," one of the most practical distinctions in the history of semantics.

Next comes *On Writing Well* by editor and author William Zinsser. This inspirational mentor of writers was taking poetry lessons at the age of ninety, and continued to coach students though he was blind. His book sold a million copies over thirty years. It makes one point: Too much writing in America is riddled with clutter. We can't see the beautiful and important stuff because of all the weeds. He shows how to cut them.

Let's read *The Souls of Black Folk* by W. E. B. Du Bois. Few works over the last century have illuminated the experiences of Black Americans with such persuasive insight. This book is a forerunner leading the way for all the important writing about race in the decades to come. His explanation of the "two-ness" of Black experience is a model for all conceptual writers.

I am proud of a former student, Mónica Guzmán, the author of the recent book *I Never Thought of It That Way.* The work begins with a startling scene on election night 2020, when she and her mother wonder if they can watch the presidential election results together. Her parents, Mexican immigrants who value law and order, voted twice for Trump, while their daughter despises what he stands for. That dilemma launches her discussion of how we can communicate as citizens across ideological differences.

Widely regarded as one of the most influential writers on the pandemic, Ed Yong is the author of many books and articles for *The Atlantic*. We will learn much from *I Contain Multitudes: The Microbes Within Us and a Grander View of Life*. I have quoted Yong at length on the methods and mission of science writing. In this text we will be able to visit the place where scientific information meets splendid literary style.

When it comes to the use of plain English in the public interest, there is no more important writer and teacher than Bryan A. Garner. A lexicographer and legal expert, Garner has given us *Legal Writing in Plain English*, in which he says, "The best approach [in writing] is to be relaxed and natural sounding. That tone bespeaks confidence. It shows that you're comfortable with your written voice." Most of the lessons and exercises in the book work not just for those in the legal profession, but for all public writers.

My best colleagues are reflective practitioners and practical scholars. This second group would benefit from the work of language scholar Helen Sword, a book titled *Stylish Academic Writing*. I'm tempted to write that Sword's pen is mighty. "There is a massive gap," she argues, "between what most readers consider to be good writing and what academics typically produce and publish." We all will learn from her examples of scholars who write in a clear and compelling public voice.

There may be no more productive and versatile public writer in America than Michael Lewis. There is no topic — from innovative baseball strategies to the causes of the Great Recession — that Lewis cannot tackle with style and insight. Let's read *The Fifth Risk* about the erosion of the federal bureaucracy under Trump. It asks the question "What are the consequences if the people given control over our government have no idea how it works?"

While my wife was receiving treatment for breast cancer, I found the book *Radical: The Science, Culture, and History of Breast Cancer in America.* The author, Kate Pickert, is a journalist and teacher who also experienced the disease. We can read it as a model for those who want to interlace personal experience with public issues and social history.

It was encouraging while writing *Tell It Like It Is* to find a new book by teacher and author Zachary Michael Jack. It is titled *The Art of Public Writing*, and it is the first time I saw the phrase "public writing" elevated to such prominence. It is a text filled with practical advice and good examples.

If ever there was a book title for the moment it would be *High Conflict: Why We Get Trapped and How We Get Out.* Amanda Ripley is the veteran journalist who could no longer stand to watch the dark news of the day. With compelling examples and innovative strategies, she challenges us to "rehumanize" our opponents. She honors those who can revive "curiosity and wonder," even as they fight for what they know is right.

We cannot ignore the language of conspiracy theorists and its spellbinding effects. To help us understand, we'll read *Cultish: The Language of Fanaticism* by Amanda Montell.

Must-reading is *These Truths*, a startling history of the United States by Jill Lepore, who happens to be both a history professor at Harvard and a staff writer for *The New Yorker.*

If *Tell It Like It Is* works for you, you may be interested in my books that preceded it, all published by Little, Brown. Here they are in chronological order:

Writing Tools: 55 Essential Strategies for Every Writer
The Glamour of Grammar: A Guide to the Magic and Mystery of Practical English

Help! For Writers: 210 Solutions to the Problems Every Writer Faces
How to Write Short: Word Craft for Fast Times
The Art of X-Ray Reading: How the Secrets of 25 Great Works of Literature Will Improve Your Writing
Murder Your Darlings: And Other Gentle Writing Advice from Aristotle to Zinsser

Keep reading and writing in the public interest, brothers and sisters of the word. If you find mistakes that require correction, or have other comments to offer, you can find me on Facebook, on Twitter (@RoyPeterClark), or via email: rclark@poynter.org.

ACKNOWLEDGMENTS

The story goes like this: It is 2005 and I have pitched an idea for a book to a New York literary agent named Jane Dystel. It did not pan out. It was the third pitch that did not pan out. "What else you got?" she said. The rest is history — and mystery. *Writing Tools* was published in 2006. The book, translated into Danish, German, Arabic, Chinese, and Russian editions, just marked a twenty-fifth paperback printing, with some 300,000 copies in print in all formats. Five books with Jane would follow, bringing total copies to more than half a million. And now you have book number seven.

But I am leaving out a key player. When we were trying to sell *Writing Tools*, Jane introduced me to a new editor at Little, Brown — a grand old publisher, I learned, known for publishing the poetry of Emily Dickinson. The editor — now vice president, publisher, and editor-in-chief — at LB was Tracy Behar. Tracy has gifts that most writers dream of in an editor: the ability to see the unfulfilled potential in a work and to inspire writers to do their best. When I started my teaching career in 1974, I thought of myself as a good reader, a young scholar, and a smart-alecky kid from Long Island. It took many years before I thought of myself as a writer. It took Tracy Behar to turn me into an author.

To both Jane and Tracy, I send my deepest gratitude and love.

St. Petersburg, Florida, my home since 1977, is a City of Writers. Thanks to my friends and colleagues at the Poynter Institute and the news organization it owns, the *Tampa Bay Times,* winner of fourteen Pulitzer Prizes. Special thanks go to Neil Brown, Kelly McBride, Jessi Navarro, Tom Jones, Ren LaForme, Daniel Funke, Katie Sanders, Andrew DeLong, Nico Guerrero, Maria Jaimes, Doris Truong, Al Tompkins, Rick Edmonds, and Paul Tash. I can't forget the influence of two wonderful Poynter pets, Maisie and Mimosa, both divas of the dog world.

Special thanks go to my editors at the *Times,* Ellen Clarke and Jim Verhulst, for finding a home for my columns in my favorite newspaper. Thanks, also, to the generous readers of those columns who—all during the pandemic—encouraged me to keep writing. Thanks to friends on Facebook and followers on Twitter for sharing your thoughts about my work with civility and good humor.

Thanks to the writers, teachers, scholars, and critics whose influence found its way into this book. They include Tom French, Kelley Benham French, Mary Claire Molloy, Kenny Irby, Jason Moyer, Eric Deggans, Colette Bancroft, Lori Roy, Mallary Tenore, Diana Sugg, Maureen McDole, Bob Devin Jones, Joe Hamilton, Paul Wilborn, Tom Hallock, Jay Rosen, Peter Meinke,

Helen Wallace, Holly Slaughter, Tom Huang, Mario Garcia, Roger Black, Michelle Hiskey, Jan Winburn, Paul Kramer, Mark Kramer, Lucy Calkins, Chip Scanlan, and Gloria Muñoz.

Thanks to Alsace Walentine, Candice Anderson, and all the great women of Tombolo Books. At a crucial time, you created a wonderful progressive space for readers and writers of all ages. You are true champions of literacy, democracy, and community. Keep selling all those banned books.

During the writing of this book, I lost two of my closest friends and mentors: Don Fry and Stuart Adam. I feel their presence, along with that of other late colleagues and teachers, including James Carey, Rene Fortin, Gene Patterson, Merl Reagle, and Donald Murray.

I cannot express deeply enough my gratitude to my alma mater, Providence College. Thanks for honoring me in countless ways for more than fifty years. And cheers to the basketball team reaching the Sweet Sixteen during March Madness the very month I finished this manuscript. Go Friars!

Thanks for all those at Little, Brown who helped me tell it like it is. This includes Karina Leon, Betsy Uhrig, Katherine Akey, Fanta Diallo, Jayne Yaffe Kemp, Christine Cox, and the eagle-eyed Kathryn Rogers, who helped me fulfill my potential as a clear and honest writer. Special thanks to Keith Hayes for another remarkable cover design, his seventh on my behalf. It continues to be an honor to say to potential readers: "Please judge this book by its cover!"

Among havens during the pandemic years were coffee shops in St. Pete that offered lattes and nourishment in safe open-air environments. The baristas and servers have become some of our closest friends and provided wonderful spaces to meet old friends and make new ones, as we all tried to make sense of a world in turmoil. These spaces are Uptown Eats, Craft Kafe, The Banyan, Black Crow Coffee Co., Book + Bottle, Kahwa Coffee, and Gypsy Souls Coffee House. Special thanks go to Erica Allums, who started it all.

That leaves my family. Thanks to my brothers Vincent and Ted. Thanks to my in-laws, the members of the Major family. Thanks to my three daughters, Emily, Lauren, and Alison, and the wonderful families they have given to us.

This book is dedicated to my wife, Karen Major Clark. During the writing of this book, we celebrated our fiftieth wedding anniversary. Because of the pandemic—and because she was in the middle of chemotherapy—we canceled a celebration, just as countless Americans had to forgo the normal rituals of life. That did not stop our daughters and friends from creating an automobile parade in the neighborhood, with golden signs and balloons. Rather than renew our vows in a church, our pastor, Msgr. Robert Gibbons, said he would come over to the house to bless our wedding rings. In a mild panic, I realized I had misplaced my ring, so I drove to Walmart. They had only one band in my size: a silver-plated beauty I bought for $38 and wear proudly to this day.

Karen's biggest contribution to my effort was to encourage me to convert our living room and dining room into a home office where I could work safely during months of quarantine. This is the first book I have ever written from home, and although I missed the benefits of my usual Poynter routines, I learned new skills that I am proud to share with all public writers.

PERMISSIONS ACKNOWLEDGMENTS

The author is grateful to all the writers and publications who are quoted as examples of excellence in public writing. Thanks to these publications in particular: the *New York Times*, the *Washington Post*, *The Atlantic*, *The New Yorker*, the *Tampa Bay Times*, Bloomberg, and the Associated Press.

Thanks to Aiden Segrest and to the publication of Lakewood High School in St. Petersburg, Florida, for permission to reprint his column on what it was like to get COVID.

Thanks to Mary Claire Molloy for permission to reprint her story on the killing of a man during social justice protests. Versions were published by Jeremy Hogan in The Bloomingtonian, the *Indianapolis Star*, and *USA Today*. Thanks to all for permissions.

Thanks to the *Tampa Bay Times* for providing numerous examples of excellent public writing used as models in this book. In particular for permission to reprint "What Is a

'Very Good Job' on Coronavirus Deaths?" by Cass Sunstein, distributed by Bloomberg News.

Thanks to the website of the Poynter Institute (www.poynter.org) for publishing early versions of several chapters. Thanks also to Daniel Funke and his editors at PolitiFact for permission to reprint and repurpose the chapter on misinformation during the pandemic.

The title of this book, *Tell It Like It Is*, was inspired by a song performed by Aaron Neville in 1966. The song was written by Lee Diamond and George Davis.

INDEX

ABOUT THE AUTHOR

By some accounts, Roy Peter Clark is America's writing coach, devoted to creating a nation of writers. A Ph.D. in medieval literature, he is widely considered the most influential writing teacher in the rough-and-tumble world of newspaper journalism. With a deep background in traditional media, Clark has illuminated the discussion of writing on the internet. He has gained fame by teaching writing to children and has nurtured Pulitzer Prize–winning authors such as Thomas French and Diana K. Sugg. He is a teacher who writes and a writer who teaches.

For more than four decades, Clark has taught writing at the Poynter Institute, a school for journalism and democracy in St. Petersburg, Florida, considered among the most prominent such teaching institutions in the world. He graduated from Providence College with a degree in English and earned his Ph.D. from Stony Brook University. In 2017 he was given an honorary degree from his alma mater and invited to deliver the commencement address at Providence's centennial celebration.

In 1977 he was hired by the *St. Petersburg Times* (now the *Tampa Bay Times*) as one of America's first writing coaches and worked with the American Society of News Editors to improve newswriting nationwide. He has taught writing at news organizations, schools, businesses, nonprofits, and government agencies in more than forty states and on five continents.

Among his clients at Poynter: the *New York Times*, the *Washington Post*, National Public Radio, *National Geographic*, *USA Today*, CNN, Gannett, Microsoft, IBM, the US Department of Health and Human Services, Disney, AAA, the United Nations, the World Bank, and countless colleges and universities.

Clark has authored or edited twenty books about writing, reading, language, and journalism. Some have been translated into Spanish, Danish, German, Arabic, Chinese, and Russian. Humorist Dave Barry has said of him: "Roy Peter Clark knows more about writing than anybody I know who is not currently dead." He lives with his family in St. Petersburg, Florida, and writes regular columns for the *Tampa Bay Times*, where he is a favorite of readers who still like to hold paper in their hands.

LSC MQ 07.18.2024 #1721244635